David Edgar

WRITTEN
ON THE HEART

NICK HERN BOOKS

DAVID EDGAR

David Edgar was born into a theatre family and took up writing full
time in 1972. In 1989, he founded Britain's first graduate
playwriting course, at the University of Birmingham, of which he
was director for ten years. His stage adaptations include Albie
Sachs's *Jail Diary*, Charles Dickens's *Nicholas Nickleby* (both for
the Royal Shakespeare Company), Gitta Sereny's biography of
Albert Speer (National Theatre), Julian Barnes's *Arthur & George*
(Birmingham Repertory Theatre), and Henrik Ibsen's *The Master
Builder* (Chichester Festival Theatre). He has written two
community plays for Dorchester: *Entertaining Strangers* and *A
Time to Keep* (with Stephanie Dale). His original plays for the RSC
include *Destiny*, *Maydays*, *Pentecost* and *The Prisoner's Dilemma*.
Other recent plays include *Daughters of the Revolution* and
Mothers Against (Oregon Shakespeare Festival and Berkeley
Repertory Theatre), *Playing with Fire* (National Theatre) and
Testing the Echo (Out of Joint). He is the author of *How Plays
Work* and President of the Writers' Guild.

ABOUT THE ROYAL SHAKESPEARE COMPANY

The Royal Shakespeare Company at Stratford-upon-Avon was formed in 1960 and gained its Royal Charter in 1961. This year we celebrate 50 years as a home for Shakespeare's work, the wider classical repertoire and new plays.

The founding Artistic Director, Peter Hall, created an ensemble theatre company of young actors and writers. The Company was led by Hall, Peter Brook and Michel Saint-Denis. The founding principles were threefold: the Company would embrace the freedom and power of Shakespeare's work, train and develop young actors and directors, and crucially, experiment in new ways of making theatre. There was a new spirit amongst this post-war generation and they intended to open up Shakespeare's plays as never before.

The impact of Peter Hall's vision cannot be underplayed. In 1955 he had premiered Samuel Beckett's *Waiting for Godot* in London, and the result was like opening a window during a storm. The tumult of new ideas emerging across Europe in art, theatre and literature came flooding into British theatre. Hall channelled this new excitement into the setting up of the company in Stratford. Exciting breakthroughs took place in the rehearsal room and the studio day after day. The RSC became known for exhilarating performances of Shakespeare alongside new masterpieces such as *The Homecoming* and *Old Times* by Harold Pinter. It was a combination that thrilled audiences.

Peter Hall's rigour on classical text became legendary, but what is little known is that he applied everything he learned working on Beckett, and later on Harold Pinter, to his work on Shakespeare, and likewise he applied everything he learned from Shakespeare onto modern texts. This close and exacting relationship between writers from different eras became the fuel which powered the creativity of the RSC.

The search for new forms of writing and directing was led by Peter Brook. He pushed writers to experiment. "Just as Picasso set out to capture a larger slice of the truth by painting a face with several eyes and noses, Shakespeare, knowing that man is living his everyday life and at the same time is living intensely in the invisible world of his thoughts and feelings, developed a method through which we can see at one and the same time the look on a man's face and the vibrations of his brain."

A rich and varied range of writers flowed into the company and continue to do so. These include: Edward Albee, Howard Barker, Edward Bond, Howard Brenton, Marina Carr, Caryl Churchill, Martin Crimp, David Edgar, Peter Flannery, David Greig, Tony Harrison, Dennis Kelly, Tarell Alvin McCraney, Martin McDonagh, Rona Munro, Anthony Neilson, Harold Pinter, Stephen Poliakoff, Adriano Shaplin, Wole Soyinka, Tom Stoppard, debbie tucker green, Timberlake Wertenbaker and Roy Williams.

The Company today is led by Michael Boyd, who is taking its founding ideals forward. His belief in ensemble theatre-making, internationalism, new work and active approaches to Shakespeare in the classroom has inspired the Company to landmark projects such as *The Complete Works Festival*, *Stand up for Shakespeare* and *The Histories Cycle*. He has overseen the four year transformation of our theatres, he has restored the full range of repertoire and in this birthday year we are proud to invite the world's theatre artists onto our brand new stages.

The RSC Ensemble is generously supported by THE GATSBY CHARITABLE FOUNDATION and THE KOVNER FOUNDATION

The RSC is grateful for the significant support of its principal funder, Arts Council England, without which our work would not be possible. Around 50 per cent of the RSC's income is self-generated from Box Office sales, sponsorship, donations, enterprise and partnerships with other organisations.

Supported by
ARTS COUNCIL ENGLAND

NEW WORK AT THE RSC

We are a contemporary theatre company built on classical rigour. We commission playwrights to engage with the muscularity and ambition of the classics. We have recently re-launched the RSC Studio to resource writers, directors and actors to explore and develop new ideas for our stages. We invite writers to spend time with us in our rehearsal rooms, with our actors and practitioners. Alongside developing their own plays for our stages, we invite them to contribute dramaturgically to both our main stage Shakespeare productions and our Young People's Shakespeares.

We believe that our writers help to establish a creative culture within the Company which both inspires new work and creates an ever more urgent sense of enquiry into the classics. The benefits work both ways. With our writers, our actors naturally learn the language of dramaturgical intervention and sharpen their interpretation of roles. Our writers benefit from re-discovering the stagecraft and theatre skills that have been lost over time. They regain the knack of writing roles for leading actors. They become hungry to use classical structures to power up their plays.

The RSC Literary Department is generously supported by THE DRUE HEINZ TRUST.

This production of *Written on the Heart* was first performed by
the Royal Shakespeare Company in the Swan Theatre,
Stratford-on-Avon, on 27 October 2011. The cast was as follows:

GEORGE ABBOT	**Bruce Alexander**
CHAPLAIN	**Jamie Ballard**
WILLIAM TYNDALE	**Stephen Boxer**
RICHARD THOMSON/ WILLIAM LAUD	**Paul Chahidi**
LANCELOT ANDREWES	**Oliver Ford Davies**
LAURENCE CHADERTON/ ARCHDEACON	**James Hayes**
JOHN OVERALL	**Jim Hooper**
PAINTER/PRISON KEEPER	**Youssef Kerkour**
SAMUEL WARD	**Joseph Kloska**
HENRY, PRINCE OF WALES	**Sam Marks**
LORD'S WIFE/ LADY ALLETTA CAREY	**Annette McLaughlin**
MARY CURRER	**Jodie McNee**
CHURCHWARDEN/WORKMAN	**Ian Midlane**
YOUNG CATHOLIC PRIEST/ SIR JOHN HARINGTON	**Mark Quartley**
CLERK	**Daniel Stewart**
SIR HENRY SAVILLE/LORD	**Simon Thorp**
CHARLES, DUKE OF YORK	**Hal Hewetson** **Christopher James Kingdom** **Charlie Waters**

All other parts played by members of the Company.

Directed by	**Gregory Doran**
Designed by	**Francis O'Connor**
Lighting Designed by	**Tim Mitchell**
Music by	**Paul Englishby**
Sound Designed by	**Jonathan Ruddick**
Company Dramaturg	**Jeanie O'Hare**
Translations by	**Reglindis de Ridder (Flemish)** **Ralph Williams (Greek/Hebrew/Latin)**
Company Text and Voice work by	**David Carey**
Additional Company Movement by	**Struan Leslie**
Assistant Director	**Thomas King**
Music Director	**John Woolf**
Casting by	**Helena Palmer** CDG
Children's Casting by	**Barbara Roberts** CDG
Production Manager	**Rebecca Watts**
Costume Supervisor	**Sarah Bowern**
Company Manager	**Jondon**
Stage Manager	**Suzanne Bourke**
Deputy Stage Manager	**Lorna Seymour**
Assistant Stage Manager	**Chris Priddle**

MUSICIANS

Soprano	**Anna Bolton**
Soprano	**Alexandra Saunders**
Tenor	**Mitesh Khatri**
Tenor	**Matthew Spillett**
Bass	**Lewis Jones**

This text may differ slightly from the play as performed.

JOIN US

Join us from £18 a year.

Join today and make a difference

The Royal Shakespeare Company is an ensemble. We perform all year round in our Stratford-upon-Avon home, as well as having regular seasons in London, and touring extensively within the UK and overseas for international residencies.

With a range of options from £18 to £10,000 per year, there are many ways to engage with the RSC.

Choose a level that suits you and enjoy a closer connection with us whilst also supporting our work on stage.

Find us online

Sign up for regular email updates at **www.rsc.org.uk/signup**

Join today

Annual RSC Full Membership costs just £40 (or £18 for Associate Membership) and provides you with regular updates on RSC news, advance information and priority booking.

Support us

A charitable donation from £100 a year can offer you the benefits of membership, whilst also allowing you the opportunity to deepen your relationship with the Company through special events, backstage tours and exclusive ticket booking services.

The options include Shakespeare's Circle (from £100), Patrons' Circle (Silver: £1,000, Gold: £5,000) and Artists' Circle (£10,000).

For more information visit **www.rsc.org.uk/joinus** or call the RSC Membership Office on 01789 403 440.

THE ROYAL SHAKESPEARE COMPANY

WRITTEN ON THE HEART

David Edgar

To Fiona and her family

Characters

LANCELOT ANDREWES, *Bishop of Ely, fifty-five*
GEORGE ABBOT, *Bishop of London, late forties*
SAMUEL WARD, *scholar, mid-thirties*
JOHN OVERALL, *Dean of St Paul's, fifty-one*
A WORKMAN
LAURENCE CHADERTON, *Master of Emmanuel, Cambridge, seventies*
RICHARD THOMSON, *scholar, c. forty-five*
SIR HENRY SAVILLE, *Warden of Merton, Oxford, sixty*
MARY CURRER, *maidservant, twenty*
WILLIAM TYNDALE, *translator, forty-one*
A YOUNG CATHOLIC PRIEST, *early twenties*
A PRISON KEEPER, *Flemish, forties*
A PAINTER
AN ARCHDEACON, *the older priest, now seventy*
A CHAPLAIN, *the younger Andrewes, now thirty-three*
A CLERK, *thirty-six, later forty-three*
A CHURCHWARDEN
A LORD
HIS LADY
SIR JOHN HARINGTON, *courtier, eighteen*
HENRY, PRINCE OF WALES, *sixteen*
CHARLES, DUKE OF YORK, *ten*
LADY ALLETTA CAREY
WILLIAM LAUD, *thirty-five*

Setting

The play is set in Ely House, Holborn, in the autumn of 1610, and at various points and places in the preceding seventy-five years.

Note on the text

A forward slash (/) in the text indicates the point at which the next speaker interrupts.

The translations were made by Reglindis de Ridder (Flemish) and Ralph Williams (Greek, Hebrew, Latin). The English translations of lines in foreign languages are in square brackets, and are not intended to be spoken.

The play can be performed by fourteen actors.

This text went to press before the end of rehearsals and so may differ slightly from the play as performed.

ACT ONE

Prologue

The chapel of Ely House, Holborn, some time towards the end of 1610. Upstage, the altar table is covered with a Turkey carpet and an altar cloth; there are two candlesticks, a cross, a cushion on which lies a prayer book, and a chalice. When we see it again in Act Two, we'll realise that the chapel is being furnished and decorated, so some pieces of furniture are incomplete or unupholstered. BISHOP LANCELOT ANDREWES, *fifty-five, has flung himself on the altar, muttering and shouting, full of passion and despair.*

ANDREWES. O base and loathsome sinner that I am.

I have forsworn God's law.
I have returned like a dog to its vomit or a sow to her mire.
I know, O Lord, the plague of my heart.
O Lord, with all my heart would I return to you.

ANDREWES *hears something, and turns from the altar.*

Who are you? Do I know you? Are you there?

Scene One

The lobby of Ely House. In fact, earlier the same afternoon. Two clerics stand waiting. SAMUEL WARD, *in his thirties, of Sidney Sussex, Cambridge, has a pile of unbound folio sheets, some books, other papers and notes, and an escritoire. He has a gentle face, a soft beard, and a stammer. Also the imposing and impatient figure of* GEORGE ABBOT, *forty-eight, Bishop of London. There is no furniture.*

ABBOT. I had thought this business to be done.

WARD. Ind-d-deed, my lord.

A WORKMAN *enters with a stool, which he puts down, none too graciously.* ABBOT *gestures to* WARD, *indicating that one stool won't be enough. The* WORKMAN *goes out.*

ABBOT. I am waited for at Westminster.

WARD. Yes, my lord?

ABBOT. The Bishop knows that we are here?

WARD. The B-B-Bishop is at p-prayer.

ABBOT. At prayer.

Enter JOHN OVERALL, *Dean of St Paul's, in his early fifties.*

OVERALL. My lord, good afternoon.

ABBOT (*surprised and displeased*). Why, Master Dean.

OVERALL (*handing his wet cloak to* WARD). I had presumed this matter to be long since resolved.

ABBOT. Yes. As had I.

OVERALL. I have hurried here, from other duties.

ABBOT. You are not alone.

The WORKMAN *comes on with a chair. He realises – and* ABBOT *indicates – that this will not be enough either. He plonks the chair down and leaves.*

OVERALL. So, you are not yet in conference?

ABBOT. The Lord Bishop is engaged in higher things.

OVERALL. Did not the Bishop call this conference?

ABBOT. No, but his house was deemed the most convenient. Or, the least / inconvenient –

OVERALL. So, who –

He is interrupted by the entry of LAURENCE CHADERTON, *early seventies, Master of Emmanuel College, Cambridge; followed by* RICHARD THOMSON, *forties, a fellow of Clare College.* CHADERTON *shakes his coat free of rain.*

CHADERTON. Masters, forgive me. I have ridden here, from Cambridge, in the rain. I must own that I cannot rightly see a need for this assembly. The few remaining points at contest can,

I'm sure, be reconciled without your trouble. My Lord of
London, I am sure you could be otherwise employed. The Dean
of St Paul's, similarly. You know Master Thomson? Master
Ward, you have the list?

OVERALL. The list?

CHADERTON. Like Master Thomson, Master Ward is one of the
twelve scholars who are revising our great work, at Stationers'
Hall.

OVERALL (*to* ABBOT). I had thought him of the Bishop's
household.

THOMSON. And have been for many months.

ABBOT. I had thought: 'our great and now completed work'.

The WORKMAN *re-enters with a bench which he dumps and
leaves. Firmly,* WARD *sits on the bench, putting down his
papers, books and escritoire. He finds a list of Biblical texts,
hands it to* CHADERTON, *and arranges the papers on the
bench beside him.*

CHADERTON. Master Ward is of Sidney Sussex College. As
Master Thomson is of…

THOMSON. Clare College.

CHADERTON. … and myself of Emmanuel.

ABBOT. Yes, Master Chaderton. What list?

CHADERTON. Of the verses whose translation is yet to be agreed.

ABBOT. Yet to be / agreed?

CHADERTON (*looking at the list*). What is the matter with the
tenth of Romans?

WARD. '*Homologeitai.*' 'Confessing' or 'acknowledging'.

CHADERTON. Ah. And second Samuel?

WARD. '*Na'ameta li meod.*' 'D-delectable' or 'very p-pleasant'.

CHADERTON. Oh, yes?

ABBOT (*to* THOMSON). Clare College.

THOMSON. And I hold a living at Snailwell, near Newmarket. By
favour of my lord of Ely.

CHADERTON. Yes, where is my lord of Ely?

OVERALL. At his devotions.

ABBOT. As is his custom for five hours a day.

CHADERTON. Two Thessalonians?

> WARD *finds the text as the* WORKMAN *crosses the stage, carrying an unupholstered kneeling stool.*

OVERALL. So where would you be now, my lord?

ABBOT. Westminster.

OVERALL. Ah. The King's finances.

ABBOT. No, that is the Commons' interest. I am occupied – I would be occupied – in deliberation of the measures needful to arrest the growth of recusancy, oaths and sabbath breaking.

OVERALL. So the land is suddenly afflicted with a plague of Sunday sports and swearing?

CHADERTON (*to* WARD). And the tenth of Mark?

> WARD *searches through the folios for a reference.*

ABBOT. You are not persuaded of the papist threat?

WARD. 'Thy faith hath healed thee' or 'thy faith hath saved thee'.

OVERALL. I am persuaded of the greater threat, of separatists, who would sunder up the Church into a thousand fragments.

ABBOT. Is that so.

OVERALL. For if popery is tyranny, then is not puritanism anarchy?

ABBOT. Well, that's / a pretty saying –

OVERALL (*knowing perfectly well*). What think you to the Spanish match, my lord?

ABBOT. What think you to it.

OVERALL. As the King does.

ABBOT. And how's that?

OVERALL. Why, that for Prince Henry to take a Catholic Queen might usher in an age of peace and concord across Europe.

THOMSON. The Prince says that two religions cannot lie in the one bed.

CHADERTON. And we might say, that if Henry the Eighth divorced himself from Rome, it's a pretty thing for Henry Ninth to wed back into it. (*To* WARD.) Sixteenth of Matthew?

WARD (*pointing on the list*). Yes, Master Chaderton.

OVERALL. What's that?

WARD. 'That thou are P-P-eter and upon this rock / I will – '

OVERALL. ' – I will build my church.' And what error / may be found there?

CHADERTON. It is proposed that 'church' be changed to 'congregation'.

Pause.

ABBOT. Is it now.

CHADERTON. I need not advertise the use to which the traditional rendering of that verse is put by those for whom St Peter is the first Pope and his church a basilica in central Italy.

The WORKMAN *crosses again, this time with a carpet over his shoulder.*

OVERALL. Master Chaderton, you were among those at the conference at Hampton Court six years ago –

THOMSON. Six years.

OVERALL. – when His Majesty proposed this new translation?

CHADERTON. I think it was proposed by others. But the King approved it.

OVERALL. And did not His Grace Archbishop Bancroft, long may he live and prosper, issue rules for the translation?

CHADERTON. He did, certainly.

OVERALL. Insisting that the ordinary Bible of the Church – (*Gesturing at the folio sheets.*) the Bishops' Bible, was to be followed, and 'so little altered as the truth of the original permitted'?

ABBOT. So he said.

OVERALL. And that those words be kept that have traditionally been used? 'Priest' not 'elder', 'the church' not 'congregation'? And that where there is dispute, the words be kept which are most common to the ancient fathers?

CHADERTON. Those were the rules six years ago.

OVERALL. Six years ago, indeed. And yet, lords, we are gathered, or you might say, rather – dragged here, while our greater duties fall into neglect. The King's treasury is bare, the Spanish match is in contention, and both superstition – seemingly – and separatism – manifestly – stalk the land. While we adjudicate between 'acknowledge' and 'confess', weigh 'heal' and 'save', and distinguish – if distinction may be drawn – between 'very pleasant' and 'delectable'.

SIR HENRY SAVILLE *has entered. He is sixty, the only Bible translator not in holy orders.*

SAVILLE. Yes, Master Dean, like you I had thought this luggage to be boxed.

Takes WARD*'s list and looks at it.*

Yet, as we think us ready to depart the house, there are yet more chattels lurking in the further corners of the closet. Which for all their diligence, our revisers at the Stationers' Hall have failed yet to pack away. And so I saw fit to gather some of us together, scarred veterans of this campaign, who did indeed consider us well shot of this most godly work. Is this the list of texts in contest?

WARD (*not knowing* SAVILLE). Yes, my…

ABBOT (*helping* WARD). Sir Henry Saville.

CHADERTON (*introducing*). Master Ward.

THOMSON (*helping* WARD). Of Merton Oxford and of Eton School.

OVERALL. It's a marvel he can tear himself away.

SAVILLE. But for today, a humble member of my Lord Bishop's translating company.

OVERALL. Or as we'd thought and hoped, a *former* member of / my lord's –

SAVILLE. And who better to adjudicate upon these weighty matters than – (*Sudden thought.*) Where is my Lord of Ely?

OVERALL. He is yet to grace us with his presence.

ABBOT. He is praying.

THOMSON. As he does five hours a day.

CHADERTON. And why my Lord of Ely?

SAVILLE. Bishop Andrewes is a man of noted piety and exemplary scholarship.

THOMSON. And great preferment.

SAVILLE. Surely. He has done and will yet do great service to the state against both papistical and puritan excess. Who knows to what further heights he may aspire.

OVERALL (*with a glance at* ABBOT). Who knows indeed.

SAVILLE. Hence the suggestion that, on these few matters yet in contest, we should seek his judgement.

ABBOT. Whose suggestion?

OVERALL. Sir Henry, I am told you lecture on astromony. And yet you are indifferent whether the Sun goes round the Earth or the Earth goes round the Sun.

SAVILLE. I have an opinion on / the matter.

ABBOT. How does this speak / to –

OVERALL. So may these matters prove indifferent too.

SAVILLE. Yet I fear there is a strong view that the time has now come for this great work to be done. As soon as may be. A view expressed, I must say, in the sharpest terms.

OVERALL. By whom?

CHADERTON. I think Archbishop Bancroft asks himself, when in due time he is called to meet his maker, at what great doing he will point his crook.

THOMSON. In 'due time'.

OVERALL. So this is his 'suggestion'?

SAVILLE. Did I say 'suggestion'? More of a command.

OVERALL. From Bancroft?

SAVILLE. From the King.

Pause.

ABBOT. Master Dean had raised the matter of the rules.

SAVILLE. Which, as I understand it, are themselves a matter of dispute.

OVERALL. As you understand it?

CHADERTON. As I indicated, Master Dean.

OVERALL. And the King will take this?

SAVILLE. The King will take – will listen to – the best advice from this assembly.

During this, MARY CURRER, *a maidservant, enters with a tray of mugs.*

THOMSON. And notably my Lord of Ely.

SAVILLE. On whose judgement he is ever happy to rely.

OVERALL (*to* ABBOT). And you, my lord? You are happy that 'the church' gives way to 'congregation'? My Lord Bishop?

ABBOT. No, but I would be rid of 'penance' and 'confessing'.

OVERALL. So 'congregation' is from Master Chaderton.

CHADERTON. And from the Greek.

SAVILLE. On which my Lord of Ely will adjudicate.

WARD. But, sirs, whatever my Lord B-B-Bishop says…

OVERALL. Yes, Master Ward? 'Whatever your Lord Bishop says?'

THOMSON, *who has seen* MARY, *coughs. The* COMPANY *turns to her.*

MARY. Sirs, I am asked by my Lord Bishop to present his salutations. He apologises that he does not rightly know why you are come.

Annoyance.

ABBOT. He does not rightly know why / we –

MARY. But he is right content to see you.

CHADERTON. That is most / generous –

MARY. At four o'clock.

SAVILLE. At four o'clock?

MARY. He has instructed drink shall be provided.

ABBOT (*making to leave*). Even so.

CHADERTON. So, Master Ward?

WARD (*his courage having left him*). I...

CHADERTON. 'Whatever my Lord Bishop...'?

ABBOT *turns back to* WARD.

WARD. I m-m-meant, sir, merely... that if this business is not
rightly done, then I fear that t-t-ten years hence we may find
ourselves not m-m-matched to Spain but in its thrall.

Slight pause.

And that if we render elders 'priests', in fifteen years we may
consign the godly to the fire. That if congregation's 'church',
repentance 'penance' and believe 'confess', then in t-t-twenty, t-
tyranny will st-t-talk the land and our civil peace lie shat-terred.
I meant, I mean, we do not deal with one archbishop's work but
the fates of kings and nations, in this matter, Master Dean.

Pause.

OVERALL. With that, sir, I agree. But I draw an opposite
conclusion. That if indeed the word of scripture is – literally –
the Word of God, then what may he make of it who finds
'church' and 'priest' in his old Bible, but not in the new? Will he
think that God has changed His mind? And, if so, what lies
shattered then?

SAVILLE. We have spoken of Archbishop Bancroft. Who
proffered Rome a policy of toleration, if the Pope would but
withdraw his blessing on those who would, in his name,
overthrow our king. It went unheeded, and, as a consequence,
gunpowder was laid beneath the Palace of Westminster. A
timely flourish, Master Ward.

He takes a mug, drinks it off.

I will see you in an hour.

He goes. OVERALL *is looking something up in his own, octavo Latin text.*

ABBOT. I wonder at Sir Henry's purpose in this business.

OVERALL. Oh, he is ever mindful of great offices.

CHADERTON. Sir Henry is Provost of a school in Berkshire.

OVERALL. I was not referring to *his* office.

ABBOT. So, to which?

OVERALL. One senior to yours, my lord.

CHADERTON. That's a narrow picking.

ABBOT. And there is no vacancy.

OVERALL. For now. (*To* WARD.) Well, if our work is to preserve the peace, let's to it: Is Acts Three listed?

WARD. No, Master D-D-Dean.

OVERALL. In verse nineteen, might we change 'repent' to 'do ye penance'? As it is in St Jerome.

He waits to see that WARD *is noting it down, which he does.*

CHADERTON. Then, one of Titus, five? Might 'ordain priest' be 'choose elders'?

OVERALL. Then, 1 Timothy 6:5, shall we change 'separate thyself' to – say – 'withdraw'?

OVERALL *smiles at his conceit, and withdraws, refusing the offered drink.*

CHADERTON. I wonder at the Bishop.

ABBOT. Which Bishop?

CHADERTON. I had not thought my Lord of Ely unlured by temporal ambitions.

ABBOT. Oh, for what?

CHADERTON. For the office senior to yours, my lord.

Slight pause.

ABBOT. Perhaps Bishop Andrewes is less confident than Sir Henry that the King will reward the adjudicator in this case.

(*To* WARD.) The second book of Kings. Chapter twenty-three. When King Josiah breaks the idols, make it 'images'. Shall we not say what we mean?

He goes out. A moment.

CHADERTON. It is pleasing that the Bishop takes such dislike to images.

WARD. On d-d-doctrine, he is of our faction.

THOMSON. Yet I venture that he has his eye on the same prize.

CHADERTON *gives a non-committal gesture. He is about to go out, but has a second thought.*

CHADERTON (*to* WARD). In ten of John, the Saviour speaks of the faithful as a 'fold'. Make that a 'flock'. (*To* THOMSON, *in explanation.*) A flock: a congregation of God's creatures. A fold: a means by which they are confined.

He shakes his head at the profferred beer, and goes out.

THOMSON. Will you too be about your business, Master Ward?

WARD. In fact, I have no urgent, or p-p-particular…

THOMSON. I am sure that you have pressing matters to attend to. A whole hour.

WARD *is a little annoyed at being bounced into going, but nonetheless stands.* THOMSON *gestures to see the list, which* WARD *hands over and goes out.* THOMSON *goes to take a mug of beer from* MARY. *She then turns to go out with the tray.*

You may put it down.

She puts down the tray.

MARY. So what's your pressing business, sir?

THOMSON. To see your master.

MARY. He's at prayer.

THOMSON. Then I will wait.

He sits on the bench. MARY *is making to go.*

So do you know of these great men?

MARY. No, sir.

THOMSON. The say-what-we-mean man is the Bishop of London.

MARY. Fancy that.

THOMSON. Though his ambitions may run even higher.

MARY. What's higher than the Bishop of all London?

THOMSON. The Archbishop of all Canterbury. And thereby, all England.

MARY. But 'there is no vacancy'.

THOMSON. Archbishop Bancroft's dying.

Slight pause.

So naturally the future of his Church is a matter of contention.

MARY. How?

THOMSON. Whether its reform has gone too far, which is the view of the Dean of St Paul's, or 'thus far but no further', that of Bishop Abbot, or 'not far enough', that of Master Ward.

MARY. And what faction are you, sir?

THOMSON. My faction is my patron's.

MARY. And what's that?

THOMSON. Your master is ever quiet in his opinion.

MARY. Yet the flock-not-fold man thinks he might want Canterbury too.

THOMSON *smiles at her.*

But this is surely not the purpose of your gathering?

THOMSON. Indeed not. We are making a new translation of the scripture.

MARY. All of it?

THOMSON. From Genesis to Revelation.

MARY. And there be need for such a work?

THOMSON. Good question.

THOMSON *finds a text in the folio of the new Bible, and reads it:*

'And the serpent said unto the woman: "Ye shall not surely die."
And the woman saw that the tree was good for food, and
pleasant to the eyes.'

*He picks up one of the books: in fact, William Tyndale's
Pentateuch.*

MARY. That is the story of our first mother and her disobedience.

THOMSON. 'Then said the serpent unto the woman: "Tush ye
shall not die." And the woman saw that it was a good tree to eat
of, and lusty unto the eye.'

MARY. That's different words.

THOMSON. Which like you better?

MARY. The second.

THOMSON. Why?

MARY. It's common speech.

THOMSON. The first is ours. The second was made by William
Tyndale, the first man to render it from Hebrew into English,
over eighty years ago.

MARY. Why don't you keep it how he wrote?

THOMSON. It's 'common speech'.

MARY. You'd change God's Word?

THOMSON. Every translator changes letters, words and
sentences.

MARY. Not Tyndale, truly. Was he not forced to flee from England,
pursued by the servants of Sir Thomas More, the agent of the
Antichrist?

THOMSON. How do you know this?

MARY. I read it in the Book of Martyrs.

THOMSON (*a little surprised*). You know that Thomas More was
put to death?

MARY. For treason.

THOMSON. Do you ever read More's writings?

MARY. Tush, no.

THOMSON. There's a book of his, which describes a place he calls '*nova insula utopia*'.

MARY. That's Latin.

THOMSON. You don't have Latin?

MARY. And I'm glad of it, if I needs must read Sir Thomas More.

THOMSON. In this book he writes of an imaginary island where all property is held in common.

MARY. Not like England, then.

THOMSON. Like no place on earth. There is plurality of doctrine, priests may be of either sex, and marry, and there are no lawyers.

MARY. Heaven.

THOMSON. In imagination.

MARY. We have married priests.

THOMSON. Some of the customs of this – island, may seem strange to us.

MARY. Oh, yes?

THOMSON. Or even lewd.

MARY. Oh, yes?

THOMSON. For example, before marriage – (*In Latin.*) '*Mulierem enim, seu virgo seu vidua sit, gravis et honesta matrona proco nudem exhibet.*' ['A grave and honest matron shows the woman, whether she be virgin or widow, naked to the wooer.']

MARY. I tell you, I've no Latin.

THOMSON. As men are not so wise as to choose a woman only for her character, but also for her comeliness, they should be cautious not to take such an important matter on mere trust. So… before marriage… a grave and honest matron presents the woman, whether she be virgin or widow, naked to the wooer.

Slight pause.

So what do you think to that?

MARY. I think it good enough for an imaginary island.

She goes to pick up and take out the tray of beer.

THOMSON. What is your name?

MARY. It's Mary Currer.

THOMSON. Might you let yourself be so presented, Mary?

MARY. What, to my future husband?

THOMSON smiles, shuts the book, puts it down before her, and places a coin on top.

THOMSON. Thus far and no further.

MARY. And you a godly man.

THOMSON. My will is free. And so is yours.

He taps the coin. MARY *understands the offer, and lifts her skirt, to show herself to him. He gestures for her to turn. She does so, lifts her skirt again, and sees* ANDREWES *enter. She drops her skirts.* THOMSON *stands.*

Lord Bishop.

ANDREWES. Master Thomson. I thought my visitors had gone.

THOMSON. I wished – I had some business.

ANDREWES. Evidently.

THOMSON. May I speak of it?

ANDREWES. Yes, if you wish.

THOMSON. The living you procured for me.

ANDREWES. In – Snailwell?

THOMSON. Yes. I've planted a vine there.

ANDREWES. I trust it will bring forth good fruit.

THOMSON. It already has, my lord. I have had a barrel of it sent for you.

ANDREWES. I quiver with anticipation. Nonetheless…

He makes to go.

THOMSON. Snailwell too is most delectable.

ANDREWES. So I am assured.

THOMSON. But it furnishes me but eighty pounds a year.

ANDREWES *sees the list and picks it up. Pause.*

ANDREWES. Yet I still wonder at the needfulness of this convention. I had thought this tree to be full-fruited long ago.

THOMSON. It but awaits your pruning hook, my lord.

ANDREWES. My pruning hook?

THOMSON. We are gathered for your adjudication on these matters.

ANDREWES. I would... I would it were not so.

A difficult pause.

THOMSON. The Dean of St Paul's fears that if popery leads on to tyranny, then puritanism will bring anarchy.

ANDREWES. Both pose great dangers, evidently, to the Church.

THOMSON. Whose future governance was a matter of much talk, my lord. In the event that the Archb–...

Another hard pause. ANDREWES *looks hard at the list.*

ANDREWES. This is the list of texts yet unagreed?

THOMSON. It is, my lord.

ANDREWES (*reading*). Mark 10:52?

THOMSON. 'Thy faith hath healed thee.' From the Rheimish version.

ANDREWES. And the contention?

THOMSON. That it might be better rendered as 'thy faith hath saved thee'. Faith not a physic but a gift.

ANDREWES. Indeed.

THOMSON. Master Chaderton calls the Rheimish text the 'Romish' text.

ANDREWES. And yet for all its papist prejudice, it is right on Mark 10:52. (*To* MARY.) There is a – pile of Bibles on the writing table in the library. Please fetch them.

MARY. Yes, my lord.

She glances at the coin, decides to leave it there, bobs and goes out. A sticky pause.

THOMSON. It was not her doing.

ANDREWES. I had not thought it so.

THOMSON. Why not?

ANDREWES. *Semper idem*, [it is ever thus] Master Thomson. I hear reports of your conduct at Clare College.

Re-enter WARD. He is dripping wet. He doesn't immediately see ANDREWES.

THOMSON. Why, Master Ward.

WARD. Master T-Thompson, I've returned. It is cold and raining and I have no other business out of d-d-doors. Pressing or otherwise.

ANDREWES. Then you must await your fellows here.

WARD *(sees ANDREWES)*. Lord B-B-Bishop.

ANDREWES *(referring to the list)*. 1 Timothy 6:5?

WARD. Paul's injunction to the just to sep-p-parate themselves from those who cleave not to the wholesome words of Christ.

ANDREWES. And the matter?

WARD. The Dean of St Paul's favours 'withdraw'.

ANDREWES. And what is your opinion?

WARD. I… consider it a matter of ind-d-difference.

ANDREWES *(with the list)*. But not all of these contentions, surely?

Slight pause.

WARD. No.

THOMSON. Master Ward has had a premonition. He fears that, if Acts Three counsels 'penance' rather than 'repentance' then the godly shall be massacred and tyranny will stalk the land.

ANDREWES *looks to* THOMSON.

ANDREWES. So not so much a premonition, as a prophecy. It would be good for us to pay it heed.

He makes to go. Turning back:

Master Ward, did I not see you once in a play at Cambridge? Some years ago?

WARD. Yes, sir, it's possible…

ANDREWES. I fear that plays are little to my taste.

WARD. I have not trifled in such manner since.

ANDREWES. You played – Dame Virtue?

WARD. Dame Goodly Thinking.

ANDREWES. Evidently. I admired it greatly.

He picks up the coin from the Bible and hands it to THOMSON.

Master, you should make haste back to Newmarket, to tend your vine. After all, your living is but eighty pounds a year.

THOMSON. My lord, I am of your party in these matters.

ANDREWES. Nonetheless.

ANDREWES *goes out with the list and the folios.*

WARD. What is the m-m-matter?

THOMSON. It is a question of how far to go.

WARD. To Newmarket?

THOMSON. To Canterbury.

WARD. What, Bishop Andrewes / has declared –

THOMSON. No, truly. God forbid, that a man of such – such goodly thinking – should fall prey to temporal ambition.

MARY *enters with a pile of books.*

MARY. I have the Bishop's books.

THOMSON. He's in his chapel.

WARD *sees the top book in the pile, takes it, looks at it, and shows it to* THOMSON.

WARD (*to* THOMSON). What's this?

THOMSON. It's the Rheimish text of the New Testament.

WARD. The Romish text.

THOMSON. He asked for it.

WARD. Then I will t-t-take it to him.

He takes the pile of books from MARY *and goes out.*

MARY. What is 'the Rheimish text'?

THOMSON. It's a Bible translated into English by a group of exiled Romanists in France.

MARY. So it's an ill translation.

THOMSON. It is full of Latin words.

MARY *makes to go.*

Forgive me.

MARY *looks back at him.*

So what like you to read?

MARY *turns to go.*

In the English tongue?

MARY. God's Word.

THOMSON. Just that?

MARY. And of the men who died that I might read it in my tongue.

THOMSON. You mean… ?

MARY. You know them.

THOMSON. Even so.

Pause.

MARY. Why, then, in King Henry's time, little Thomas Bilney, priest and martyr, who the night before his burning placed his finger in the candle till it blackened to the knuckle, that he might be brave before the fire. And in the dark time of Queen Mary, Bishop Hooper, who at the last did beat his breast until one hand fell off and the other spat and splattered with the blood and fat that dripped down from his fingers. And Archbishop Cranmer, who abjured but then renounced his treachery to Christ, putting out the hand that had first signed his recantation to the flames to burn up like a coal before the people. And goodly Agnes Potten and Joan Trunchfield, worthy William Pikes and godly Alice

Driver, all of Ipswich, the last who drove her father's plough before she was condemned for reading of the Scripture, and who blessed the chain they put about her neck to burn her as God's neckerchief. So we might read the book you seek to change today.

THOMSON. You learn this in the Bishop's library?

MARY. No, in my father's house. My grandmother was burnt before his face. It's how I learn to read.

Slight pause.

That and the English Bible.

Scene Two

High mass in a great cathedral in Flanders, 5 October 1536. Lit from high windows. A YOUNG PRIEST *among the* CELEBRANTS. *The* CHOIR *sings a motet, with the text:*

CHOIR. *Gaude gloriosa dei mater virgo Maria.* [Rejoice in the glorious Mother of God, the Virgin Mary.]

The YOUNG PRIEST *rises and walks, stumbling a little, away from the cathedral towards a cell in Vilvoorde Castle, near Brussels. In contrast with the cathedral, it is dark, grey, sparse and cold. An unlit stove. In a threadbare coat,* WILLIAM TYNDALE, *forty-one, sits at a table on which are books and papers. His* KEEPER *admits the nervous* YOUNG PRIEST. *The* KEEPER *only speaks Flemish.*

KEEPER (*in Flemish, to* PRIEST). *Ge zijt zeer laat. Het kasteel sluit normaal om zes uur. Na het donker laten we hier geen buitenstaanders meer toe.* [You are very late. The castle closes at six o'clock. No outsiders are allowed here after dark.]

YOUNG PRIEST (*in Latin, to* TYNDALE). *Quid dicit?* [What does he say?]

TYNDALE. He says you're very late.

YOUNG PRIEST (*in Latin*). *Morari paululum necesse fuit.* [I was delayed a little.]

KEEPER (*in Flemish*). *Ge moet binnen het kwartier vertrekken.* [You must leave in fifteen minutes.]

TYNDALE. You must leave in a quarter of an hour.

YOUNG PRIEST (*in Latin*). *Post quartam horae partem!* [After a quarter of an hour!]

TYNDALE (*in Flemish, to the* KEEPER). *Hij vindt dat erg kort.* [He thinks that is a very short time.]

YOUNG PRIEST (*in Latin, to the* KEEPER). *Tu me vocavisti.* [You asked for me.]

TYNDALE. *I* asked for you.

KEEPER (*in Flemish*). *Ik mag niemand / binnenlaten* – [I am not required / to admit anyone –]

YOUNG PRIEST (*in Latin, to* TYNDALE). *Cur me vocavisti tu?* [Why did you ask for me?]

TYNDALE. I knew that someone would be sent. I have, God knows, seen enough. But I have not heard or spoken in my tongue for eighteen months. And I wished to do both whilst I still have tongue to speak it.

Slight pause. The YOUNG PRIEST *acknowledges, in a slightly embarrassed way.*

And they send you.

The KEEPER *sits on a stool by the door.*

YOUNG PRIEST (*in Latin*). *Ad me venit...* [To me came...] I was approached by the Procurator General.

TYNDALE. Ah.

YOUNG PRIEST. I was the only priest available.

TYNDALE. I see.

YOUNG PRIEST. I am, I fear, no theologian.

TYNDALE. But you are a priest. And I presume a scholar?

YOUNG PRIEST. My father felt it best I should take holy orders. And now that the Church is in such travail from King Henry...

TYNDALE. He sent you for your safety to Louvain.

YOUNG PRIEST (*puts out his hand*). You are William Tyndale.

TYNDALE. You will shake my hand?

YOUNG PRIEST. Why, should I not?

TYNDALE *shrugs, shakes* YOUNG PRIEST*'s hand.*

TYNDALE. Do you know why I am here?

YOUNG PRIEST. In prison? Why –

TYNDALE. No, in Flanders.

YOUNG PRIEST. You fled from England some – nine years ago?

TYNDALE. Eleven. Why?

YOUNG PRIEST. You were in hazard of the law for heresy.

TYNDALE. No, I wished to make that which I had tried but failed to make in England.

YOUNG PRIEST. What, rebellion?

TYNDALE. No, a thing which by much labour, and much hazard, and some flights upriver on the Rhine, and a shipwreck off the Dutch coast, and the loss of everything, and the abandonment of work for risk of capture, I finished and then saw to print.

YOUNG PRIEST. You mean your English / Bible.

TYNDALE. The New Testament and the first books of the old.

YOUNG PRIEST. Which you then smuggled into England.

TYNDALE. To be burnt at Smithfield, by a Cardinal.

YOUNG PRIEST. By order of the King.

TYNDALE. And then I am arrested by the forces of the Antichrist.

YOUNG PRIEST. By the Holy Church.

TYNDALE. And I am incarcerated here, for heresy. And you are come to 'save me'.

YOUNG PRIEST. For which I would needs see your face. Is there no light?

TYNDALE (*in Flemish, to the* KEEPER). *Hij vraagt om licht.* [He asks for light.]

The KEEPER *shrugs, with a mordant little smile.*

(*To the* YOUNG PRIEST.) Twelve months ago, I wrote to the governor of the castle, asking for a woollen shirt and leggings, and a coat to replace my old one, which was – is – worn and thin. Also a Hebrew Bible and a grammar and a dictionary, so I might pass my time in study. And lamplight for the evening.

YOUNG PRIEST. And were these requests granted?

TYNDALE. I have the books.

YOUNG PRIEST. But not the means to read them after dark.

He goes to the table and looks at TYNDALE*'s papers.*

So you are writing?

TYNDALE. In the hours of daylight.

YOUNG PRIEST (*reading, finding a little difficulty with the handwriting*). 'He was… despised, and cast out of…'

TYNDALE. '… men's company.'

YOUNG PRIEST. It's hard to read.

TYNDALE (*in Flemish, to the* KEEPER). *De bezoeker vindt het hier nogal donker.* [The visitor remarks that it is dark.]

YOUNG PRIEST. And it's so cold.

The YOUNG PRIEST *opens the stove door to see if there's any fuel inside it.*

KEEPER (*in Flemish*). *Wat zei hij?* [What does he say now?]

TYNDALE (*in Flemish*). *Het doet er niet toe.* [It doesn't matter.]

The YOUNG PRIEST *shuts the stove door.*

YOUNG PRIEST (*to the* KEEPER). Sir, this night of all nights, your charge deserves the comfort of a lamp.

TYNDALE (*in Flemish*). *Hij zegt dat ge een lamp moet brengen.* [He says you are to bring a lamp.]

KEEPER (*in Flemish*). *Ik mag jullie niet alleen laten.* [I shouldn't leave you together.]

TYNDALE. He is not supposed to leave us.

KEEPER (*in Flemish*). *Maar ik zal een lamp gaan halen.* [But I will fetch a lamp.]

TYNDALE. But he will do as you ask.

A moment. The YOUNG PRIEST *understands, and gives the* KEEPER *a coin. The* KEEPER *goes out.*

YOUNG PRIEST. This is – Ezekial?

TYNDALE. Isaiah.

YOUNG PRIEST. You have translated all the books preceding?

TYNDALE. As I said, of the Old Testament, I have only published the Pentateuch.

The YOUNG PRIEST *looks blank.*

Genesis, Exodus, Leviticus...

YOUNG PRIEST. So, this work is...

TYNDALE. For my own comfort. What else do you know of me?

YOUNG PRIEST. It is said in Louvain, you once supped in company with a famous conjurer, but that on your order all of his enchantments failed.

TYNDALE. It was not at my order, but in my presence. If his tricks succeeded elsewhere, I know not.

YOUNG PRIEST. One imagines, if they did not, he would lack employment / as a conjurer –

TYNDALE. Whereas the conjuration I have been ever keen to halt is masses. Kneeling and kissing holy relics. Incense, candlewax and holy water, or as we say, 'Pope's piss'. Babbling and braying. Miracles and mumblings of penances and purgatory. By priests who cannot tell the Ten Commandments or who gave us the Lord's Prayer, but whose only study is fee-gathering and licking arses. So, you are come to save my soul?

Pause.

Presuming that my body is beyond salvation.

The YOUNG PRIEST *sits, opens his satchel, takes out papers.*

YOUNG PRIEST. This which follows is needful that you do recant. To save your soul.

TYNDALE. You have come prepared.

YOUNG PRIEST. Would you expect me to come otherwise?

TYNDALE. I meant, so uncertain of your argument, that like a lazy actor you have not learnt your script.

YOUNG PRIEST. It is necessary, first, that you recant as ungodly and malicious the false teachings of the lecherous nun-marryer, arch-heretic and traitor, Luther.

TYNDALE. Oh. Which teachings?

The YOUNG PRIEST *needs to consult his notes; sometimes, this involves a bit of a scrabble.*

YOUNG PRIEST. Uh… Rejecting saintly intercession. And…

TYNDALE. The sacraments?

YOUNG PRIEST. All but three of the holy sacraments.

TYNDALE. All but two. (*Waiting and then prompting.*) And, purgatory?

YOUNG PRIEST. Yes.

TYNDALE. Which is not an ancient doctrine but a recent, fond and covetous imagining, to persuade the gullible that by the proceeds of their purse they may more speedily process to Heaven. Second?

YOUNG PRIEST. Second, that you must confess the needfulness of good works to the achievement of salvation.

TYNDALE. I assert that '*sola fides justificat apud Deum*'. (*To help.*) We are justified before God…

YOUNG PRIEST. … by faith alone.

TYNDALE. And not by paternosters, penances or prayers to posts.

The YOUNG PRIEST *trying to find the right note.*

(*Prompting.*) And if we are not saved by our good works…

YOUNG PRIEST. Uh…

TYNDALE. What is to keep men from a life of sin?

YOUNG PRIEST. To which / you answer?

TYNDALE. To which I answer that it is not the fruit makes the tree good, but the tree the fruit. 'Shall we sin, because we are not under the law, but under grace? God forbid!'

Slight pause. YOUNG PRIEST *gives a wan smile.*

(*Prompting.*) But, nonetheless, have we no need / of priests to –

YOUNG PRIEST. But, nonetheless, save for priests, shall not false heresies be preached, shall not prayer and fasting be neglected?

TYNDALE. Ah! You have read the hell-hound Thomas More.

YOUNG PRIEST. Do not the followers of Luther, of which you are chief, join together in foul lechery, abhor good governance and rise against their rulers?

TYNDALE. You have not read my books. I am no commonwealther. I say that all men should obey the king.

YOUNG PRIEST. Even if they urge us to disobey God's law?

TYNDALE. Yes, for evil rulers are a rod and scourge by which God chastises us.

YOUNG PRIEST. Does not the King of England burn your books?

TYNDALE. He burns God's books.

YOUNG PRIEST. And you would kiss the brand?

TYNDALE. I have said a hundred times that I would suffer what he will, even unto death, if he would grant a bare text of Scripture in the English tongue to be put forward to his people.

YOUNG PRIEST. Any text, or your text?

TYNDALE. My text is a bare text in the English tongue. But, yes, any text.

YOUNG PRIEST. For, third, you must recant your text as heretical, false and corrupt.

TYNDALE. I must break the glass wherein we see God's face?

YOUNG PRIEST. Yes, if that glass is warped.

TYNDALE. How warped?

YOUNG PRIEST *scrabbling for this section of his notes.*

YOUNG PRIEST. By terms which are unseemly in the testament.

TYNDALE. For example?

The YOUNG PRIEST *is scrabbling.*

(*Prompting.*) Does not the serpent…?

YOUNG PRIEST. Does the serpent not tell tempted Eva: 'tush ye shall not die'?

TYNDALE. Should the serpent be more seemly?

YOUNG PRIEST (*from his notes*). And are there not, further, words made ill in meaning. 'Congregation', where the proper word is 'church'? 'Love' for the virtuous affection we call 'charity'.

TYNDALE. Oh, you think that 'agape' means merely 'charity'?

YOUNG PRIEST. And do you not take words and phrases crudely from the Hebrew, without finding proper English renderings, and thus to make a nonsense in our tongue?

TYNDALE. For example?

YOUNG PRIEST. 'Fat *of* the land.' 'Cool *of* the day.'

TYNDALE. It is a true rendition of the Hebrew.

YOUNG PRIEST. And the sweet music of our English is made raucous and obscure.

TYNDALE. How so?

YOUNG PRIEST. 'A – tone – ment'. 'Scape – goat'. 'Beauty – ful'.

TYNDALE. Again, / I say –

YOUNG PRIEST. Why not our good word 'beauteous'? And for that matter, what fool would suffer a fool gladly? What eye has scales? What is the apple of an eye? What might a man die but his death? Shall sin pay wages? 'God forbid', indeed.

TYNDALE. And if the English Bible had 'ordain' for 'choosing', 'church' for 'congregation', 'charity' for 'love'. Then might it be freely read?

YOUNG PRIEST. Why should it not be?

TYNDALE *picks up a Latin Bible and thrusts it at the* YOUNG PRIEST.

TYNDALE. Find me bishops. Find me the Pope. Find me holy relics or the seven sacraments. Oh. Find me purgatory.

Slight pause.

And tell me why, if the bishops are so blithe for a Bible in the common tongue, why it is still in law a burning matter to possess it? And, for that matter, no hand raised to save me, an English subject imprisoned in a foreign land?

The YOUNG PRIEST *takes the testament.*

YOUNG PRIEST. And the truth that lies here, may all men find it?

TYNDALE. Any ploughboy. If in a language he may understand.

YOUNG PRIEST. We have no need of learning to unlock its meaning?

TYNDALE. As Paul writes, when he was a child, he spake and understood as one, but when he was a man, he put childishness away. Seeing no longer in a glass, as a dark speaking, but face to face, in God's true light.

YOUNG PRIEST. In which light any man may read it?

TYNDALE. Any honest man.

YOUNG PRIEST. And who may judge if he be such a man? And if any man makes what he fancies of God's word, might he not make nothing? Might he not cut off the branch on which he sits?

TYNDALE. What, if that branch is the love of Jesus Christ, in his blood spilled on the cross? (*Quotes.*) For, 'though I could prophesy, and understand all knowledge, and though I gave my body even that I burned, and yet had no love… it profiteth me nothing.'

YOUNG PRIEST. But is there no love in priests? Or comfort in a company? Is there not succour in a ceremony, and does not what you call 'braying' fill the soul? And if we cannot read the sense, of the hard places, must we sit silent with our book in the evening darkness, fearful and alone? And what if, when we look into our heart, we find it empty?

TYNDALE. Oh, no. No. For in the word of Christ, that he came into the world to save sinners, of which I am the chief, there is such comfort and such sweetness and such love that a man may never feel alone again. The love that Mary Magdalen did feel for Christ, that she did inflame and swell with it, that she could not abide but it must burst out from her body… For we write not a dead law with ink and parchment but a living law which only love and mercy understand. And he that has not that written on his heart, shall never understand it; no, though all the angels were to teach him.

YOUNG PRIEST. So you will step gladly to the fire.

TYNDALE. I shall not burn.

YOUNG PRIEST. I…

TYNDALE. My fate is to be strangled and my body burnt. It is a 'generosity'.

YOUNG PRIEST. You sound as if… the sharper penalty might be… to your liking.

TYNDALE. 'The fire shall try every man's work, what it is.' But no. Though I would not disdain to follow so many godly martyrs on that path.

Pause.

Is your work done?

YOUNG PRIEST. Well, I have finished.

TYNDALE. You can go back to your studies.

YOUNG PRIEST. I have failed.

TYNDALE. Then you have succeeded.

YOUNG PRIEST. And… tomorrow?

TYNDALE. My body will return to the dust whereof it came.

YOUNG PRIEST. And your soul?

TYNDALE. Will sleep until the day of judgement.

YOUNG PRIEST. That is your belief?

TYNDALE. That is God's truth.

YOUNG PRIEST. Perhaps… it might be… I have no idea if such a thing is possible.

TYNDALE. A stay?

Pause.

On condition I recant 'that which is needful'?

Clearly impossible. The YOUNG PRIEST *puts his papers back in his satchel.*

YOUNG PRIEST. When they searched me, they asked me of these writings. I said they were to save your soul. They said I would need more than writings.

He stands. TYNDALE *stands.*

TYNDALE. Then I thank you for your pains and hope you do not think this a bootless journey or a wasted study.

YOUNG PRIEST. No, I do not.

TYNDALE. For in truth, God made me evil-favoured in the world, rude and slow-witted.

YOUNG PRIEST. I do not think so. Will you carry on your work tonight?

TYNDALE. By God's grace, if I have a candle.

YOUNG PRIEST. So how far have you reached?

Pause.

TYNDALE. Reached?

YOUNG PRIEST. In the Old Testament.

TYNDALE. I told you. I have already published Genesis to Deuteronomy.

YOUNG PRIEST. Then it is Joshua, Judges, Samuel?

TYNDALE. Ruth, Samuel. What do you mean?

YOUNG PRIEST. I saw the bundle in the stove. Have you yet reached One Kings? Two Kings?

TYNDALE. Two Chronicles.

YOUNG PRIEST. Nine further books. What will be done to them?

TYNDALE. What is done to me.

YOUNG PRIEST. So then, where must I take them?

TYNDALE. What d'you mean?

YOUNG PRIEST. Where must I take your papers?

TYNDALE. You would take them?

YOUNG PRIEST. Yes.

TYNDALE. To burn them?

YOUNG PRIEST. As will happen if they stay. To give them to whoever is your will.

TYNDALE. And to betray he that receives them?

The YOUNG PRIEST *makes for the stove.*

YOUNG PRIEST. Your keeper will return at any time.

TYNDALE. As I was betrayed?

YOUNG PRIEST. Master Tyndale, if I am to / undertake –

TYNDALE *stands in the* YOUNG PRIEST*'s path.*

TYNDALE. Why do you offer this?

YOUNG PRIEST. Why, does that signify?

TYNDALE. It does to God.

YOUNG PRIEST. Then, so the ploughboy may read Joshua and Chronicles.

TYNDALE. And you?

YOUNG PRIEST. That I may read Joshua and Chronicles?

TYNDALE. That you account yourself saved by the blood of Jesus Christ?

YOUNG PRIEST. Why, surely.

TYNDALE. And that blood alone.

YOUNG PRIEST. That – first. Master Tyndale –

TYNDALE. And do you condemn as guilty of the grossest heresy Sir Thomas More and the bishops and the Pope?

YOUNG PRIEST. Master, let me save your papers.

TYNDALE. Priest, let me save your soul.

YOUNG PRIEST. You will forbid me that I take your papers, save that I declare the Church to be the Antichrist?

TYNDALE. 'For the belief of the heart justifies, and to acknowledge with the mouth makes the man safe.'

YOUNG PRIEST. And what is 'acknowledge' in the Latin?

TYNDALE. It's '*confessio fit*'.

YOUNG PRIEST. Then I acknowledge in my mouth, believing in my heart.

TYNDALE. And truly? Freely?

YOUNG PRIEST. Yes, if you will it. May I –

TYNDALE. It is not my will.

YOUNG PRIEST. It is not your will alone. So may I. Please.

But as TYNDALE *stands aside, the* KEEPER *enters with a lit candle and a bag of logs, which he tosses down by the stove.*

KEEPER (*in Flemish, to* TYNDALE). *Hier is een kaars. De kasteelheer heeft me de toelating gegeven de stoof aan te steken.* [There is a candle. I have permission from the governor to light the stove.]

He puts the candle on the table.

TYNDALE. The governor has granted leave to light a fire. (*In Flemish, to the* KEEPER.) *Dank u wel, mijnheer de bewaker, maar ik kan het vuur zelf wel aansteken.* [Thank you, Mr Keeper. But I can light the fire myself.]

KEEPER (*in Flemish*). *Nee, nee, laat mij dat maar doen.* [No, no, I'll light it.]

TYNDALE. He says he'll light it.

The KEEPER *opens the stove, sees the bundle, and takes it out.*

KEEPER (*in Flemish*). *Hier is aanmaakhout.* [There's kindling.]

TYNDALE. He's found kindling.

The KEEPER *opens the bundle of papers.*

YOUNG PRIEST. Let me help you.

TYNDALE (*in Flemish, to the* KEEPER). *Hij zegt: 'ik zal u helpen'.* [He says, 'let me help you'.]

KEEPER (*in Flemish*). *Als hij per se wil.* [If he wants to.]

TYNDALE. If you want to.

YOUNG PRIEST (*kneeling down by the* KEEPER). You've smudged your face.

KEEPER (*in Flemish, to* TYNDALE). *Wat zegt hij?* [What does he say?]

TYNDALE (*in Flemish, to the* KEEPER). *Ge hebt uw gezicht smerig gemaakt.* [You've smudged your face.]

The KEEPER *wipes his face, and looks at his hand. Then he starts to scrumple up the papers.*

YOUNG PRIEST. Say something then blow out the candle.

TYNDALE. Say what?

YOUNG PRIEST. Oh, anything. Isaiah.

TYNDALE. 'He was despised and cast out of men's company.'

TYNDALE *blows out the candle. The* KEEPER *looks round, and can see* TYNDALE *shrug. The* KEEPER *gets up, goes to the table, taking out a steel and flint.*

YOUNG PRIEST. Say on.

The YOUNG PRIEST *continues to scrumple paper.* TYNDALE *carries on reading out the verses he's been translating, as if speaking in conversation, as the* KEEPER *lights the candle.*

TYNDALE. 'One that had suffered sorrow and had experience of infirmity: and we were as one that had hid his face from him. Truly he took on our diseases and / bore our sorrows.'

The KEEPER *takes the candle back over to the stove.*

YOUNG PRIEST. I think that is sufficient.

TYNDALE (*in Flemish*). *Hij vindt het zo wel voldoende.* [He thinks that is sufficient.]

KEEPER (*in Flemish*). *We zullen wel zien.* [Well, we'll see.]

He puts logs on the paper and lights them from the candle. The YOUNG PRIEST *stands, picks up his satchel.*

YOUNG PRIEST. Tell me where to take them.

TYNDALE. Take what?

The YOUNG PRIEST *opens his satchel, takes out the top sheet of 'his' papers, and reads:*

YOUNG PRIEST. 'After the death of Moses, the servant of the Lord, the Lord spoke unto Joshua.'

He puts the paper away.

I played the conjuror today. Where shall I take them?

The KEEPER *stands and looks at them.* TYNDALE *kneels.*

TYNDALE (*in Flemish, to the* KEEPER). *Ik moet even alleen zijn met mijn biechtvader.* [I need a moment, with my confessor.]

KEEPER (*in Flemish*). *Ik mag jullie echt niet meer alleen laten.* [I cannot leave you alone again.]

He sits. The YOUNG PRIEST *goes to* TYNDALE*'s table and looks at the paper.*

YOUNG PRIEST. So you have it that he was 'despised and cast out'.

TYNDALE. *'Nivzeh wachadal ishim.'* Yes.

YOUNG PRIEST. Or perhaps, rejected? Where?

TYNDALE *corrects.*

TYNDALE (*as if saying what he's writing*). John Roger, chaplain to the English House at Antwerp.

YOUNG PRIEST. 'And suffered sorrow.' He will have this printed? 'Full of sorrow'?

TYNDALE. Or 'a man of sorrows'.

YOUNG PRIEST. 'We were as one that had hid his face from him.' How do you know I won't betray him?

TYNDALE. 'We hid as it were our faces from him.' I have seen your face.

YOUNG PRIEST. And I yours. Will it be smuggled into England?

TYNDALE. By God's grace.

The YOUNG PRIEST *is moving to take the paper. The* KEEPER *stands.*

KEEPER (*in Flemish*). *Nee. Gelieve dat te laten liggen.* [No. You mustn't take that.]

The YOUNG PRIEST *looks to* TYNDALE.

TYNDALE. You mustn't take that.

YOUNG PRIEST. There's no need.

He puts down the paper and puts his hand out to TYNDALE.

You are God's freeman. May your hand be brave tomorrow. And your purpose be accomplished.

He shakes TYNDALE's *hand and goes out. The* KEEPER *follows.* TYNDALE *goes and gets the candle from the floor, by the stove. He brings it to the table, and puts it down. He looks at it. He raises his hand, as if to try it in the flame. His hand quivers, but then falls. He looks at the paper.*

TYNDALE. 'Truly, he took on our *griefs* and bore our sorrows.'

He makes the correction, then lifts the paper, as if to burn it. Another thought leads to another glance at the Hebrew and another change:

'*Makovenu.*' Bore our 'pains'.

He's finished. He burns the paper.

To Rogers then to England. And the word is out.

He blows out the candle.

Scene Three

The YOUNG PRIEST *appears, with his satchel. Before us, he changes from the twenty-year-old Catholic* YOUNG PRIEST *to a seventy-year-old, Anglican* ARCHDEACON. *Behind this, the cell changes into a small church in Yorkshire, on a summer morning in 1586.*

The church is dominated by a rood screen with a complicated history: originally, there were painted Saints, but their faces, hands and feet have been scratched out. A couple of the faces have been crudely repainted. Then, clearly, the whole screen has been whitewashed, but, last of all, the whitewash over the Saints themselves has been rubbed off. So currently we see a white screen with the Saints appearing like ghosts within it.

A PAINTER *has been painting Biblical texts onto large white panels that will be nailed over the Saints. He has finished the Ten Commandments over two panels, the Lord's Prayer and four other texts:*

' "Ye shall put nothing unto the Word which I command you, neither shall ye take ought there from." Deut., 1111,2.'

' "Then being justified by faith, we have peace towarde God through our Lord Jesus Christ." Rom., v,1.'

' "In the beginning was the Word, and the Word was with God, and that Word was God." John 1,1.'

' "And what agreement hath the Temple of God with images?" 11 Cor., vi,16.'

In this last text, there is a shadow of a correction: the word 'images' has been changed from 'idols'.

The PAINTER *reads out a text which has been dictated to him and which he has outlined on a board, to check that he's got the wording right.*

PAINTER. 'He was despised and rejected of men's company, a man of sorrows, with experience of infinity. We hid as it were our faces from him. Truly he took on our diseases and bare our sorrows.'

ARCHDEACON. 'Infirmity.' '*Bore* our sorrows.'

The ARCHDEACON *has to point at the words.*

PAINTER. I'll set about it.

He turns to go and start work on this new panel. The ARCHDEACON *looks at the second Commandments panel.*

ARCHDEACON. 'Thou shalt not commit adultery.'

PAINTER. What of it?

ARCHDEACON. It wants its 'L'.

The PAINTER *looks, breathes deeply, and goes and gets buckets of white lime and black to correct the text, as a thirty-three-year-old* CHAPLAIN *enters.*

CHAPLAIN. Archdeacon.

ARCHDEACON. Master Chaplain. The parish book?

CHAPLAIN. Nowhere to be found.

ARCHDEACON. My clerk is seeking out the churchwarden.

CHAPLAIN (*looking at the panel*). Uh – 'Adutery'?

ARCHDEACON. I know.

The PAINTER *is returning with his buckets. He starts to work on the corrections.*

Things were in this state on Sunday?

CHAPLAIN. Indeed so.

A CLERK *in his early forties pushes a* CHURCHWARDEN *into the church. The* CLERK *is in holy orders, and holding a big account book up in the air.*

CLERK. The churchwarden. And his book.

He hands the book to the ARCHDEACON.

ARCHDEACON. Good work, Master Clerk. (*To the* CHURCHWARDEN.) You are churchwarden of this parish?

CHURCHWARDEN. Aye, my lord. But –

ARCHDEACON. And this is your parish book?

CHURCHWARDEN. Truly. But the church –

ARCHDEACON. Why is it not kept in your church?

CHURCHWARDEN. Our church be afflicted with intrusion.

CLERK. You mean, by us?

ARCHDEACON. No, I believe –

CHURCHWARDEN (*the screen*). As you may well observe.

CLERK. 'Intrusion.'

ARCHDEACON. Please do sit down.

The ARCHDEACON *puts the book down as the* CHURCHWARDEN *sits. The* ARCHDEACON *opens his satchel, takes out papers, and hands some to the* CLERK, *and some to the* CHAPLAIN.

CLERK (*to himself, remembering*). The windows.

ARCHDEACON. You have met my clerk. I am Archdeacon to the see of York. This is the chaplain to the Earl of Huntingdon, Lord President of the North.

CHURCHWARDEN. Aye, I knows that.

ARCHDEACON. Because he preached here Sunday last.

CHURCHWARDEN. He did.

ARCHDEACON. Because you have no parish priest.

CHURCHWARDEN. Because our parish priest be sick.

CLERK. Hah!

ARCHDEACON. And do you know why he has returned, and brought us with him?

CHURCHWARDEN. Nay.

CLERK. Because this house is stuffed with popish trumpery.

The CHURCHWARDEN *is in despair.*

ARCHDEACON. We are here on Her Majesty Queen Elizabeth's authority, to ask you of the answers which you gave at York at the time of the late visitation. Whether they were true then, or true now. Do you understand this?

CHURCHWARDEN. Aye.

The ARCHDEACON *looks to the* CLERK.

CLERK. Item, whether all parishioners attend divine service, receiving the Holy Communion at least thrice a year?

CHURCHWARDEN. Aye.

CLERK. Whether you suffer any that peddles wares in the church at service times, or makes noise, jangles or plays the fool.

The ARCHDEACON *glances at the* CHAPLAIN, *who gives an ambivalent gesture.*

CHURCHWARDEN. Not... nay.

CLERK. Item, whether you have all things necessary for Common Prayer, especially the English Bible in the largest volume.

The CHURCHWARDEN *gestures to the church Bible on the lectern.*

ARCHDEACON. That is assent.

The CHAPLAIN *so marks it.*

CLERK. Whether you admit to communion any of your parish that cannot say by heart at least the Ten Commandments, the Articles of the Faith and the Lord's Prayer, in English.

CHURCHWARDEN. No, surely not.

The CHAPLAIN *so marks it.*

CLERK. And whether all and every mass-book, legendary and portess be utterly destroyed? Whether all tunicles, albs, stoles, pixes, paxes, sacring bells, chrismatories, censors and holy-water stoups be broken or removed? Whether your parson – when in health – do minister communion in any chalice heretofor employed at mass? And whether you have dismantled, covered and defaced all feigned images of wood or stone, or painted onto wood or stone or glass? (*To the* ARCHDEADON.) The windows.

ARCHDEACON. To which you answered?

Pause.

CHAPLAIN. That he had suffered none such to remain.

CHURCHWARDEN. I did. But then –

CLERK. But at a later time you were summoned back to York, to answer charges that painted images hitherto abused by superstitious veneration, 'Saint' Nicholas, 'Saint' Catherine and the like, whose faces had been properly scraped out, so as to stop such bowing down and lighting up and praying to, that they were restored.

CHURCHWARDEN. Not by my hand.

ARCHDEACON. And what answer did you make?

CLERK. He answered…

ARCHDEACON. Please you, Master Clerk.

CHURCHWARDEN. I answered that this work be done at night, by intruders to the church.

CLERK. And you were told to white the screen –

The CHURCHWARDEN *gestures that this was done.*

– and then to see to it the church was firmly locked against 'intruders', and then to make up tables of the Lord's Prayer and the Ten Commandments and other sober godly verses of the Scripture, and to fix them fast unto the screen so that images might be no more open to the public view.

ARCHDEACON. Which work had plainly not been done by
Sunday.

CHURCHWARDEN. But you are about it now.

CLERK. And the windows. With their images of Saints, feigned
miracles, and Christ's earthly mother.

ARCHDEACON. Truly they should be whited over.

CLERK. It is clear what happens in this house to white lime.

He goes to the PAINTER.

Is there a ladder?

PAINTER (*working*). Aye, there's a ladder.

CLERK. Then fetch it, if you please.

He notices a hammer, as the PAINTER *reluctantly goes out for
the ladder.*

ARCHDEACON. Master Churchwarden, you know rightly of the
penalties of which you stand in hazard, should it be concluded
here that you have wantonly obstructed this our holy work?

CHURCHWARDEN (*miserably*). Oh, aye.

The PAINTER *comes back in with a ladder.*

CLERK. Against the window.

The PAINTER *puts the ladder up against the window.*

CHURCHWARDEN. But, my lords...

CHAPLAIN. We are not your lords.

CHURCHWARDEN. I beg you...

CLERK (*the ladder*). Good.

CHURCHWARDEN. I have done... we have done, and stopped, all
that we...

CLERK. Clearly!

He goes and gets the hammer.

CHURCHWARDEN. But surely you must understand...

ARCHDEACON. What must we understand?

CHURCHWARDEN. The doings and undoings of our times.

The ARCHDEACON *nods to the* CLERK, *to leave the windows for a moment.*

ARCHDEACON. We follow you.

The CHURCHWARDEN *breathes deeply, then:*

CHURCHWARDEN. In King Henry's time, of blessed memory, we are enjoined to strip the statues of their clothing, and to remove the lights before them. To take down the altars and to level out the steps. Then, in the rule of his son Edward, we must smash the rood loft and pull down the images that stand below it. Rend all the primers and the legendaries, save for the English Bible. Remove all vestments, plate, and bells, and uproot the crosses from the graves. Then in the reign of his sister Mary we must put the altars up again, repaint the Saints, repurchase plate and bells and books and vestments, set back up the Latin Bible and destroy the English. Then, when our present Queen...

Slight pause.

ARCHDEACON. What of our present Queen?

The CHURCHWARDEN *nods to the parish book. The* CHAPLAIN *passes it. The* CHURCHWARDEN *opens it and reads, turning pages.*

CHURCHWARDEN. 1549: 'For removal of altar and rood loft, taking down of bells and scraping off of Saints' names: ten pounds three shillings.' 1551: 'Two shillings and threepence for taking down an image of St George.' 1555: 'Five shillings and sixpence for putting up an image of St George.' 1559: 'For the purchase of a Book of Common Prayer, three shillings and eightpence. For removing the corpus from the rood: nine shillings and five- / pence – '

CLERK. Money!

The CHURCHWARDEN *closes the book and hands it back to the* CHAPLAIN. *During the following, the* CHAPLAIN *looks through the book, and checks a couple of entries against his document.*

CHURCHWARDEN. Not just money.

ARCHDEACON. What else?

CHURCHWARDEN. You know what else.

CHAPLAIN. What else?

Pause.

CLERK. He means 'the old ways'.

Pause. The ARCHDEACON *finds a Bible in his satchel.*

ARCHDEACON. Yes. But as Paul writes, when we were children, we spoke and understood as children. But now we are men, we put all that away. No longer seeing through the dark glass of ritual and superstition, but in full light, and face to face. To know, as we are known.

He opens the Bible anywhere and thrusts it at the CHURCHWARDEN.

Find me candles. Find me holy days except the Holy Day. Find me St George or relics or the worshipping of Saints.

CLERK. Well, at least we shall no longer see their faces here.

He is heading up the ladder with the hammer as the LORD *of the Manor enters with his* LADY. *The* CHURCHWARDEN *stands.*

LORD. What's happening? What's going on? (*To the* CLERK.) What are you doing?

ARCHDEACON. Who are you?

LORD. Who are you?

ARCHDEACON. I am Archdeacon of the Diocese of York.

LADY. Another visitation!

ARCHDEACON. We are here to find out what of that which we were told was done, at the last visitation, was done truly.

LORD. What, nailing these painted texts against the screen?

ARCHDEACON. These godly texts. Who are you?

LORD. I am Lord of this manor. This is my wife. What is that man doing?

CLERK. I am going to destroy these images.

LORD (*draws his sword*). No, you shall not.

ARCHDEACON. Sir, this is a house of God.

LORD. And those are his windows.

CLERK. These windows like this screen are smeared with feigned images to which the blinded and the ignorant show worship.

LORD. What, you think folk worship windows?

ARCHDEACON. They still pray to Saints and light candles to the dead.

LORD. Not any more.

CLERK. By God's grace!

LADY. But still – they would.

Slight pause.

CLERK. Oh, would they?

LADY. As they would keep the Saints' days and the plays. Creeping to the cross at Easter. Praying to the Saints and to Christ's holy mother and the plate and the fine old Latin books and pretty things.

ARCHDEACON. What pretty things?

LORD. We are aware that such things are / no longer –

LADY. Those which the godly of this parish fashioned or had fashioned to adorn this place. To bring comfort to the faithful and colour to a ceremony.

CLERK. The godly!

ARCHDEACON. Such as?

LADY. Such as the reliquaries and decorated chalices and silver pyxes and the Sunday vestments stitched with gold thread and the velvet hangings which my father and his father gave. The pyxes broken up for balances and their gravestones dug up for a pigsty. The sacring bells hung round the necks of sheep and cows.

The CHAPLAIN *remembers something. Quickly, he checks one of the papers against the* CHURCHWARDEN'*s book.*

Gave that their souls be gathered up to Heaven and their works remembered.

Slight pause.

CLERK. All the more cause, then, for the extinction of these images.

He heads up the ladder.

LORD. Whose extinction?

CLERK. Christ's mother.

The CLERK *smashes a low window. Coloured glass falls down. The* LORD *rushes over.*

LORD. Stop that!

CLERK. And his Saints.

He smashes another window. More glass. But by now, the LORD *has his sword up against the* CLERK*'s body.*

LORD. Throw down the hammer.

ARCHDEACON. Sir, you know we act with full authority –

CLERK. What, you would kill me?

LORD. Do not try me, sir. Throw it down!

CHAPLAIN. Where is the chalice?

EVERYONE looks at him. The LORD *keeps his sword at the* CLERK*'s side.*

ARCHDEACON. What chalice?

CHAPLAIN (*to the* CHURCHWARDEN). At York you presented an inventory of the church plate, vestments and accoutrements, record of how you sold or otherwise disposed of them, and for what price.

Holds up the parish book.

They are listed in your book. But not the chalice. Nor I think a damask cope, stitched with the story of St Margaret. What happened to them?

Pause.

LORD. You preached on Sunday.

CHAPLAIN. Yes. What was my text?

LADY. Your subject was the corruption of the Church.

CHAPLAIN. I said that the clergy too easily took heed to enrich
their sons and daughters. What happened to the chalice and the
cope?

LORD. How should I know?

CHAPLAIN. I was asking the churchwarden. But I would ask a
thing of you.

LORD. As I of you.

CHAPLAIN. What is the second Commandment?

The LORD *looks quickly to the panel on which the second
Commandment is written.*

LORD. No graven images.

CHAPLAIN. And the eighth?

Before the LORD *or his* LADY*'s eye can reach the other
Commandment board, the* CHAPLAIN *knocks it down.*

LADY (*prompting*). False witness?

LORD (*taking his sword from the* CLERK*'s side*). 'Thou shalt not
bear / false witness.'

CHAPLAIN. And the twenty-second Article of Faith of the Church
of England?

LORD. Uh…

CHAPLAIN (*prompting*). What Romish doctrine is 'a fond thing,
vainly invented'?

LORD. Good works?

LADY. The seven sacraments.

CHAPLAIN. No, purgatory. (*To the* CHURCHWARDEN.) And
you tell us your parishioners take communion, thrice a year, as
no man may, save that he knows by heart the Lord's Prayer, the
Ten Commandments and the Articles of his religion. Where is
the chalice?

Slight pause.

CHURCHWARDEN. I, uh…

Pause. He flashes a look at the LORD.

I…

CHAPLAIN. Is it buried in the churchyard? Perhaps hidden in the church? Against a restoration of the old rule and 'old ways'?

He goes to the CHURCHWARDEN, *who cannot help flashing his eyes at the* LORD.

Or perhaps you could not gain a good price, with so many such treasures being sold at once. And so you kept it, in 'a place of safety'. Along, perhaps, with other items, not in the book.

Slight pause.

Knowing how prey your church is to intruders. (*To the* LORD.) It is 'thou shalt not steal'.

The LADY *nods at the* LORD, *realising that the* CHAPLAIN *is offering a deal. He sheathes his sword.*

LORD. Well. As you say.

CHAPLAIN. As I say what?

LORD. Such a thing is best kept safe, against a brisker market.

CHAPLAIN. Such *a* thing?

Slight pause.

LADY. Such things.

CHAPLAIN. Kept in a place for which you hold the key.

LORD. Precisely.

The CLERK *comes down the ladder.*

CLERK. And the cope?

CHAPLAIN. Doubtless unstitched of St Margaret and resewn up as a cushion. Will you fetch the chalice? And any other things?

Slight pause.

Or might we come and help you?

LORD. Hm.

CHAPLAIN. It is said that the Spaniard builds ships and musters sailors, for a venture to avenge his late wife's cause against our Queen, her sister. He is no doubt assured by the Jesuit spies who insolently stalk the kingdom that the 'old faith' is much held to by the common English people. And that when

the Pope instructs his followers that it is not merely a great
justice but a religious duty to rise up and slay the Queen of
England... This he imagines too. And how, when he has slain
their monarch, he'll tear out the bowels of her lords. Even
their ladies. Their bowels blown up and torn asunder. So,
item, that all of those ways and the things that mark them
shall be rent, defaced and utterly extinguished, that they may
never be restored.

LADY. Master Churchwarden. I believe my husband recollects
where he might have placed the item.

CLERK. Items!

LADY. If I can find them, will you bear them back?

Pause. The CHURCHWARDEN *nods.*

CHAPLAIN. And you will set a guard upon the church. And take
care to learn the Articles.

CLERK. And all the Ten Commandments!

LADY. Any man may mistake a number.

CLERK. Not by the law!

LORD. The puritan. A man who loves his God with all his soul and
hates his neighbour with all his heart.

He and his LADY *go out with the* CHURCHWARDEN. *The*
CLERK *goes to the* PAINTER *and gives him the hammer.*

CLERK. Nail up the texts.

PAINTER. In any pattern?

CLERK. So that the images be covered.

The PAINTER *starts nailing up the texts.*

ARCHDEACON. Good work, Master Chaplain.

The CHAPLAIN *demurs.*

I am told that the Lord President makes you busy in the prisons.
It is a stubborn Jesuit who resists you.

CHAPLAIN. I have truth on my side.

ARCHDEACON. I was once charged with such a task.

CHAPLAIN. I am sure that you succeeded.

ARCHDEACON. I failed utterly. But a great purpose was accomplished.

CHAPLAIN. What purpose?

The CLERK *has been looking at the text which the* PAINTER *read out to the* ARCHDEACON *at the beginning of the scene, which he has now painted up. He interrupts:*

CLERK. What is this text?

CHAPLAIN. It is Isaiah. But, I do not remember it as 'a man of sorrows'.

He goes to check the text in the Bible on the lectern.

ARCHDEACON. You will find, I believe, 'a man who who hath experience of sorrow'.

The CHAPLAIN *goes back to the board.*

CHAPLAIN. 'We hid – as it were – our faces from him.' So, is this your translation?

ARCHDEACON. No. Or only, in the smallest part.

CHAPLAIN. And why…?

ARCHDEACON. I once met such a man.

CHAPLAIN. We all meet him daily, in our prayers.

ARCHDEACON. Another such a man.

The CHAPLAIN *looks at him quizzically.*

Without whose teachings I would be… not the man I am.

A moment.

The text recalls us to the need for a humility. A time when the godly were not Archdeacons nor Lord Presidents but despised and cast out of men's company. For whom the unspeakable riches of God's kindness, the love that Mary Magdalen did feel for Christ, so much that it burst out from her body, was strong enough to bear them through the fire. God's – freemen.

CLERK. I am jealous of that time.

The ARCHDEACON *looks at the* CLERK.

ARCHDEACON. I am thankful for it. As I am thankful that it is no more. For, truly, only love and mercy truly comprehend the law. And he who has not that written on his heart, shall never truly come to Christ, though all the angels taught him. And God forbid it should be otherwise. Will you see this business done?

CLERK. Yes, surely.

ARCHDEACON. Good day, Master Clerk. And Master Chaplain.

He goes out.

CLERK. He was my teacher.

CHAPLAIN. How so?

CLERK. I lived in the very roaring pit of sin.

Slight pause.

CHAPLAIN. You were lucky in your schoolmaster.

CLERK. Yes. And yet.

Slight pause.

CHAPLAIN. And yet?

CLERK. We seem to tarry.

CHAPLAIN (*here and now*). We are so instructed.

CLERK. In our reformation.

CHAPLAIN. The reformation of our souls?

CLERK. The reformation of our Church.

Pause.

CHAPLAIN. It is certainly needful. As I preached on Sunday.

CLERK. What did you say of it?

CHAPLAIN. The Church? That it is slimed in simony and patronage.

CLERK. Aught else?

CHAPLAIN. Is that not sufficient?

The CLERK *gestures to the Bible at the lectern.*

CLERK. Find me bowing and the signing of the cross. Find baptism of infants, swearing oaths and Lenten fastings. Find me wedding rings. Find archdeacons.

CHAPLAIN. So, that which is not in Scripture may not be godly?

CLERK. That which is not in Scripture is idolatry.

He gestures to the Deuteronomy: 'Ye shall put nothing unto the Word which I command you, neither shall ye take ought there from.'

And for all the married priests and English Bibles, still we must wear surplices, the rags of popery. The steeplehouses echo to the jangle of the tabor and the pipe.

CHAPLAIN. The Queen likes music.

CLERK. She likes plays!

CHAPLAIN. While her popish sister Mary forbade them.

CLERK. Priests may not preach except by licence. Men must reveal the very secret thoughts and interests of their hearts.

CHAPLAIN. What are you saying?

CLERK. I am asking you to sniff the odour of the times.

CHAPLAIN. What should I smell there?

CLERK. That the discipline that should be visited upon the papists is now turned on us.

Pause.

CHAPLAIN. By 'us', you mean…?

CLERK. You are a godly man.

CHAPLAIN. If so, by His grace.

CLERK. There is… a fellowship.

CHAPLAIN. Of what persuasion?

CLERK. That of Paul in his first to Timothy.

CHAPLAIN. That is a groaning table.

The CHURCHWARDEN *enters with the chalice, and a silver pax. He sees the* CLERK *and* CHAPLAIN *speaking and remains in the shadow of the door, listening.*

CLERK. 'If any man is not content with the wholesome words of our Lord Jesus Christ... from such separate thyself.'

CHAPLAIN. Separate.

CLERK. I would not spend my life in breaking windows. I would rather be in a true communion of fellowship. Meeting not in steeplehouses but in godly houses. All in one place, and holding things in common, as every man has need.

CHAPLAIN. This is your dreaming?

CLERK. No, my doing.

CHAPLAIN. Why do you tell me this?

CLERK. To bring you to us.

CHAPLAIN. Ah.

Pause.

Your fellowship. A church separated from the Church.

Slight pause.

I fear... Despite...

CLERK. That you are not a man for us?

Pause.

CHAPLAIN. I am the man I am.

CLERK. I see.

Slight pause.

Chaplain to England's second man. Who knows to what offices you may aspire.

Pause.

CHAPLAIN (*emollient*). My vocation is as preacher. Like any Christian, I would live in fellowship with a godly gathering of freemen, withdrawn from the rough doings of the world. But I know that Spain has ships.

CLERK. I am a loyal subject to the Queen. Unless her will runs counter to the Word of God.

CHAPLAIN. I see. And if it does?

CLERK. Then I have a higher duty.

CHAPLAIN. Evidently.

CLERK. May I rely on you to keep our conversation close?

The CHAPLAIN *notices the* CHURCHWARDEN.

CHAPLAIN. Master Churchwarden.

CHURCHWARDEN. Here is the chalice. And 'other things'.

CHAPLAIN. You will sell them?

CHURCHWARDEN. Aye.

CLERK. And mark their return clearly in the book. And, naturally, their sale.

CHURCHWARDEN. I will.

He goes and writes in the book.

CLERK. Our business here is done.

CHAPLAIN. I would like to pray.

Pause.

There is no need to stay for me.

CLERK. Then, very well.

He makes to go.

CHAPLAIN. Master Clerk. What follows if a member of… such a body of freemen, were to defy the general opinion of its elders? Say, on the parsing of a text of Scripture?

CLERK. It would not be possible.

CHAPLAIN. For them to disagree? Or to be permitted to?

CLERK. For… for them to disagree. On the meaning of God's word.

CHAPLAIN. Aha.

The CHURCHWARDEN *approaching.*

CHURCHWARDEN. I have marked down the items, sir.

CHAPLAIN. Good. Farewell, then, Master Clerk.

The CHAPLAIN *nods to the* CLERK, *who goes out. The* CHAPLAIN *turns to the* CHURCHWARDEN.

Give me the chalice.

CHURCHWARDEN. Uh?

CHAPLAIN. Give me the chalice.

The CHURCHWARDEN *hands him the chalice. The* CHAPLAIN *looks at it, then opens his own satchel.*

I will gain a better price for this in York, than you will here.

He hands sovereigns to the CHURCHWARDEN.

CHURCHWARDEN. Once, there be no words in church. Now the Word be all there is.

Slight pause.

So what might you aspire to, Master Chaplain?

CHAPLAIN. Put the money to new windows.

The CHURCHWARDEN *goes out with the money. The* CHAPLAIN *stands with the chalice. Music. The thirty-three-year-old* CHAPLAIN *turns into the fifty-five-year-old Bishop of Ely,* ANDREWES, *with his white ruff and surplice, puffed sleeves, black sleeveless gown and velvet cap. At the same time, the mid-1580s Yorkshire church turns into the rich if incomplete chapel of Ely House, London, in 1610, with its grand accoutrements.* ANDREWES *looks at the chalice as if there is something on its surface. He touches it with his finger and then with his lips. He closes his eyes. Then, full of passion and despair:*

ANDREWES. O base and loathsome sinner that I am.

ANDREWES *turns, goes quickly upstage, puts the chalice on the altar and flings himself against it.*

Blackout. End of Act One.

ACT TWO

Scene One

Still in the chapel of Ely House. As if a moment after the end of the last scene, but, in fact, a moment or two after the end of Scene One. In addition to the altar and its furnishings, there is a kneeling stool, a rolled carpet, a lectern and a small writing table, on which lies the list of disputed texts and the folio Bibles. ANDREWES kneels in prayer. WARD has entered with his pile of Bibles.

WARD. My lord.

ANDREWES looks round.

ANDREWES. Why, Master Ward.

WARD. Forgive me. I have your b-b- / books.

ANDREWES stands.

ANDREWES. My books?

WARD. Which you requested.

ANDREWES. Did I not ask the maid / to bring – ?

WARD. My lord, forgive me / for –

ANDREWES. I am in your debt. And now –

WARD. But I must implore you / to address –

ANDREWES. Ah. You have some further business?

Slight pause. WARD puts down the pile of Bibles.

WARD. My business is our b-b-business.

ANDREWES (*picking up the list*). These few remaining matters of contention.

WARD. Yes.

ANDREWES. Changing 'priests' to 'elders'.

WARD. Certainly.

ANDREWES. And 'fold' to 'flock'.

WARD. The Dean of St Paul's p-p-proposes that 'repentance' should be 'penance'.

ANDREWES (*considering, a close call*). '*Metanoeo.*'

WARD. Following the p-p-practice of the Romanish translators of the University of Rheims.

ANDREWES. They of the 'longanimities' and 'conquinations'.

Intrigued by another item on the list:

What is 2 Samuel 1?

WARD. David's lamentation over Jonathan.

ANDREWES looks questioningly:

'I am – ' I think it is – 'd-distressed for thee my b-b-brother Jonathan, very pleasant hast thou been to me, thy love to me was wonderful, p-passing the love of women.'

ANDREWES. Indeed. What is the question?

WARD. As I recollect, the Geneva has 'very kind hast thou been unto me', the Matthews' Bible 'd-delectable to me wast thou exceedingly'.

ANDREWES. One sees the argument against 'delectable'.

WARD. It does not touch d-d-d-doctrine.

ANDREWES. So no one will suggest it should be 'passing the charity of women'.

WARD. No.

Pause, as ANDREWES puts down the Bible and returns to the list.

ANDREWES. Mark 10:52, however, does touch doctrine. I have no doubt that you would prefer for it to be 'thy faith hath saved thee' rather than 'thy faith has healed thee', on the grounds that '*sola fides justificat apud deum*'. But unfortunately the word is '*sesoke*' and it means 'healed'.

WARD. But surely, as a P-P-Protestant, you would wish it to be 'saved'?

ANDREWES. Master Ward, it is not a matter of what I or you might wish the words to mean, but their meaning in the Greek. And then there is the matter of Archbishop Bancroft's rules.

WARD. My lord. Archbishop B-B-Bancroft is not immortal.

ANDREWES. As much as we might pray so.

WARD. Our work will live on under his successor.

ANDREWES. As we must hope.

WARD. Whomsoever that might be.

ANDREWES. Whomsoever that might be.

WARD. Sir, you would have sat in Parliament that day.

ANDREWES. What day?

WARD. The d-day when gunpowder was found beneath it.

ANDREWES. So...

WARD. I cannot b-b-believe that you are not of our faction in this matter.

Slight pause.

ANDREWES. Which faction's that?

WARD. The faction that would change Archbishop Bancroft's rules.

ANDREWES. The puritan persuasion.

WARD. I do not hold 'puritan' to be a term of defamation.

ANDREWES. Nor I. But perhaps, distinction. Between you and me.

WARD. You have been ever a bold champion of the reformist cause. I have read your stout d-d-defence of the allegiance oath, in reposte to Cardinal Bellarmine.

ANDREWES. It is ever my desire to do the bidding of the King.

WARD. I have read your many sermons on the corruption of the Church.

ANDREWES. Ah, they are very old.

WARD. You were chaplain to the Earl of Huntingdon, a keen disciple of reform. You were a hammer to the northern papists.

ANDREWES. Not just to papists.

WARD. In d-d-determination that those whose blood was shed for the English Bible and the English Church should not have bled in vain.

Pause.

ANDREWES. Indeed. What have we suffered, in our soft and downy times?

Pause.

WARD. Well, certainly, your chapel's very fine, my lord.

ANDREWES. Ely House had fallen into some disrepair.

WARD *goes round the chapel, ending up at the altar.*

WARD. And this is your London residence?

ANDREWES. Yes, hence its name.

WARD. And do you spend much t-t-time at Ely? Ely, Cambridgeshire?

ANDREWES. Ah. I fear the Fenland air does not agree with me. But I will progress in the summer.

WARD. Perhaps you will visit us at Sidney Sussex.

ANDREWES. It would be my / pleasure –

WARD. Where at communion we sit around the table, passing the bread and wine from hand to hand, in fellowship, as if one to another.

He takes the chalice from the altar, raises it as if in a toast, and mimes drinking from it. He hands it to ANDREWES.

ANDREWES. Ah.

WARD. Ah?

ANDREWES. I have disappointed you.

WARD. I have misread your history.

ANDREWES (*putting the list down*). You have misread my inclination. I am not a Solomon to sit in judgement on your scholarship. Even less a pruning hook. My liking is not to judge but to minister and pray.

WARD. It is your habit, by repute, to p-p-pray for five hours in a day.

ANDREWES. Not every day.

WARD. Nonetheless. It's hard to think how any man might occupy five / hours…

ANDREWES. Oh, Master Ward, if five times five… If all the hours God sends.

WARD. We are all prey to the lure of temporal ambition.

ANDREWES. Ambition? Why, for what?

WARD. Why for… for the… um…

Pause.

My lord, forgive me.

ANDREWES. It is – no matter.

WARD. I too suffer from much t-t-turbulence of mind.

ANDREWES. Which to speak of is not to confess.

Pause. WARD *takes out a notebook, opens it, and hands it to* ANDREWES.

(*Reading.*) 'Vainglory. No delight in prayer. On Sunday, sleeping through a sermon. Intemperance. Excess in eating cheese and damsons. Shame in serving God.'

Slight pause.

Sleeping through a sermon. Eating cheese.

WARD. My lord, I must apologise for this / intrusion –

He turns to go.

ANDREWES. Come now. You were not to know how far this task stands from my disposition.

WARD. But, my lord, you have unique authority. If not you, who will choose?

ANDREWES. Not one who has so often chosen ill.

WARD. No more than any man.

ANDREWES. That would be enough. Even, were it so.

Pause.

I am – the man I am.

WARD. My lord, forgive me.

He turns to go.

ANDREWES. Master Ward?

WARD (*turns back*). My lord?

ANDREWES. To sleep though a dull sermon is a fault. But it is not to court hellfire.

WARD. Oh, no?

ANDREWES. And, you may, I think, allow yourself a damson.

Slight pause.

However – well, delectable.

WARD *gives a little bow and hurries out.* ANDREWES *stands a moment, then he raises the chalice. He looks at it as if there is something on its surface. He touches it with his finger and then with his lips. He closes his eyes.*

O base and loathsome sinner that I am.

ANDREWES *turns, goes quickly upstage, puts the chalice on the altar and flings himself against it.*

I have forsworn God's law.
I have returned like a dog to its vomit or a sow to her mire.
I know, O Lord, the plague of my heart.
O Lord, with all my heart would I return to you.

TYNDALE. 'And soul.' Is it not 'to turn again to thee, with all my heart and soul'? From Chronicles?

ANDREWES *turns and sees* TYNDALE.

ANDREWES. Who are you? Do I know you?

Pause.

Are you there?

TYNDALE. So this is – home.

ANDREWES. It is my home.

TYNDALE. Is nothing changed?

ANDREWES *stands.*

ANDREWES. What would you change?

TYNDALE. The altar.

ANDREWES *thinks he realises who the man is.*

ANDREWES. Ah. You have brought the altar cloth?

TYNDALE. The kneeling stool.

ANDREWES. You come to dress the kneeling stool?

TYNDALE (*at least*). No rail.

ANDREWES. To measure for the rail?

TYNDALE. There are still altar rails in England?

ANDREWES. Some. Sir, your mercy...

TYNDALE. Whose house is this?

ANDREWES. This is... the London residency of the see of Ely.

TYNDALE. There are bishops?

ANDREWES. Clearly.

TYNDALE. And chalices and cambric?

ANDREWES. Evidently.

TYNDALE. And who are you?

ANDREWES. I am... a member of the Bishop's household.

TYNDALE. Then I would fain set eyes on the Bishop.

The WORKMAN *enters with a folding stool, a pile of napkins, and a measure.*

WORKMAN. My Lord Bishop. The wainscot faldstool, to your new instruction. And the altar napkins.

TYNDALE. Altar napkins.

ANDREWES. Ah.

The WORKMAN *puts down the stool.*

WORKMAN. I am asked by the upholsterer if it is your pleasure for the kneeling stools to be faced with violet or crimson baise.

ANDREWES. Um...

The WORKMAN *puts the napkins on the altar.*

WORKMAN. And by the seamstress, to assure you that the towels and broadcloths will be here on Tuesday.

ANDREWES. Good.

WORKMAN. Is it convenient for me to measure for the rail, my lord?

TYNDALE. The rail.

ANDREWES. As you see, I am in conference.

The WORKMAN *looks round, baffled.*

WORKMAN. In conference?

ANDREWES. Yes, evidently.

The WORKMAN *works out this must be a metaphor.*

WORKMAN. Forgive me, my lord. I'll let you to your 'conference'.

He goes out.

ANDREWES. You are an effusion of my mind.

TYNDALE. And you are a Bishop.

ANDREWES. I am... the – recently inaugurated...

TYNDALE. 'Evidently.'

ANDREWES. And I am shortly to be visited by other / grave divines –

TYNDALE. Other bishops?

ANDREWES. Do you bear presentiment of a calamity? I have met men who have witnessed the dead walk.

TYNDALE. You think me a presentiment?

ANDREWES. I have known of premonitions –

TYNDALE. From the future?

ANDREWES. Once, at a playhouse, I heard a spirit cry out for revenge.

TYNDALE. Revenge?

ANDREWES. Might you be Henry Barrow?

TYNDALE. Who?

ANDREWES. A man I visited in prison – or else might you be myself?

TYNDALE. Yourself?

ANDREWES. My self. The man I was.

TYNDALE *throws his arms wide, demonstrating the poverty of his attire.*

Then am I – dead?

TYNDALE. You fear so?

ANDREWES. Or in purgatory? Should such a place…?

TYNDALE. What, purgatory? God forbid!

ANDREWES. Not that I – I myself / hold… that such a…

TYNDALE. 'For if we be dead with Christ, we believe that we shall live with / Him.'

ANDREWES. God forbid?

ANDREWES *is going to a luxuriously bound New Testament and finding a verse from Romans 6:*

TYNDALE. For 'as Christ was raised up from death by the glory of the father: even so we also should walk in a new life. For if we be graft in death like unto Him…'

ANDREWES *(who's found the verse).* '…even so must we be in the resurrection.' *(At the head of the same chapter.)* 'What should we say then? Is the law sin? God forbid.'

TYNDALE. That is my book.

ANDREWES. If you are its author.

He hands the Testament to TYNDALE.

TYNDALE. God is the author. So I am returned, to England?

ANDREWES. Not, I think, in life.

TYNDALE. And that the New Testament.

ANDREWES. Yes.

TYNDALE. And I am the translator of it?

ANDREWES. So… it would appear.

TYNDALE. In such a binding. So tricked out.

ANDREWES. Yes.

TYNDALE. But to be read, freely? Here?

ANDREWES. Yes. Now.

TYNDALE (*the other Bibles*). And these? All God's Word, in the English tongue?

ANDREWES *nods*.

My purpose is accomplished.

ANDREWES (*relieved*). And you are returned to find it so.

Pause.

TYNDALE (*reading the title page of a Bible, in some wonderment*). 'Biblia, the Bible, that is, the Holy Scripture, of the Old and New Testament.'

ANDREWES. I believe the translation of Miles Coverdale.

TYNDALE. Miles Coverdale. We worked on Deuteronomy in Hamburg. (*Reading.*) 'Faithfully translated out of Deutsche and Latin into English.'

ANDREWES. He had no Greek.

TYNDALE. Nor Hebrew. Yet still a good and godly… 1535.

ANDREWES. Yes.

TYNDALE. And this was read, in England, lawfully?

ANDREWES. There is much of yours, notably in the New / Testament.

TYNDALE. But lawfully, in England, while I had yet a year to live.

Pause.

ANDREWES. Truly, as you say. Your purpose was accomplished.

TYNDALE. Yet.

ANDREWES. Indeed.

TYNDALE. For nothing.

ANDREWES *points at Tyndale's New Testament.*

ANDREWES. No. For that.

TYNDALE. And what matter whose hand penned it?

ANDREWES (*the Coverdale*). And for that.

TYNDALE. And what happened to that hand?

ANDREWES (*pointing to the Matthew's Bible*). And then for this, published two years later, with the King's most gracious licence.

TYNDALE (*looks at the Matthew's, not knowing the name*). By Thomas Matthew?

ANDREWES (*showing other Bibles to* TYNDALE). And this, from a company of puritans – reformers – of evangelists – living in Geneva. With much marginal notation, sometimes questionable... Not to be outdone, a group of Romanists – uh, popists, papisticals – in Rheims produced a New Testament in the vernacular, full of tortured coinages – 'potestates', 'concorporate', 'resuscitation', 'allegory' – but graced with some surprisingly apt renderings. Then, for our Church of England, Archbishop Parker made a further, known as the Bishops' Bible. An unhappy work. Some extraordinary infelicities. As I remember: 'lay thy bread upon wet faces'.

TYNDALE *looks questioningly.*

'Cast thy bread upon the waters.' As we have it.

TYNDALE. 'We'?

ANDREWES. At the command of King James, six companies of 'grave divines' have been making a new translation for six years.

TYNDALE. Six companies.

ANDREWES. Fifty-four men in all.

TYNDALE. Are they your visitors?

ANDREWES. Not all fifty-four.

TYNDALE. And upon what principles?

ANDREWES (*gesturing at the Bibles*). To make that better which our predecessors left so good.

TYNDALE. Rules of consistency? The Hebrew '*waw*'?

ANDREWES. '*Waw*' is best rendered 'and'.

TYNDALE. And never 'but' or 'nonetheless'?

ANDREWES. Rarely.

TYNDALE. And the hard places?

ANDREWES. Exodus!

TYNDALE. The appointment of the temple fixtures.

ANDREWES. 'The cubit that shall be the length thereof and the breadth thereof and foursquare shall it be.'

TYNDALE. And phrase by phrase or word by word?

ANDREWES. A knotted question. So many Hebrew coinages that were once obscure and hard for us are now part of the common tongue. 'A man after his own heart.' The 'still small voice'. 'Fat of the land.'

TYNDALE. A 'small still voice'.

ANDREWES. 'Still, small', I believe.

TYNDALE. 1 Kings 19.

ANDREWES. Ah, so it must be Coverdale.

TYNDALE. No, it is not Coverdale. Did you say – Thomas Matthew?

TYNDALE *finds 1 Kings 19:12 in the Matthew's Bible.*

'And after the fire came a small still voice.'

He turns back to 1 Samuel 13:14.

'The Lord hath sought him a man after his own heart.' 1 Samuel.

ANDREWES (*taking the Matthew's from* TYNDALE). Ah. So it is a Matthew's coinage?

TYNDALE. No, it is not.

ANDREWES. But, evidently, if…

Slight pause.

In 2 Samuel, what says David on the death of Jonathan?

TYNDALE. 'Woe is me for thee my brother Jonathan. Delectable to me wast thou exceeding.'

Pause.

ANDREWES. You translated Samuel and Kings. And Chronicles.

TYNDALE. And Ruth and Judges. Who is Thomas Matthew?

ANDREWES. A false name for, I believe, an English rector, by the name of Rogers...

TYNDALE. John.

ANDREWES. Was it he who brought these books to England?

TYNDALE. I must think so.

ANDREWES. You did not place them in his hands?

TYNDALE. To those of a man who came to me in prison. And prayed with me that my purpose be accomplished.

Pause.

ANDREWES. As it is.

TYNDALE. And what became of Rogers?

ANDREWES. He made this godly book.

TYNDALE. And did hurt befall him for producing it?

ANDREWES. Not then, for it was made under the King's licence. And I am certain Rogers was in England in the reign of Edward.

TYNDALE. Edward?

ANDREWES. King Henry's heir. A zealous doer for the faction of reform.

TYNDALE. And later?

ANDREWES. Sadly, God took King Edward from us early in his age. His sister Mary, who succeeded him, was not of the reform persuasion. Much of the accoutrement and custom of the old religion was restored. Some – like good Coverdale – fled from England to Geneva. Others – unhappily – did not.

Pause.

TYNDALE. And?

ANDREWES. Your friend was burnt at Smithfield. In front of a huge crowd. His wife and many children. It is said he put his hands into the flames as if to wash them. He was, as I recall, the first evangelical – the first of many – to die for his faith in that bloody time. The year that I was born.

Pause. TYNDALE *looks at his hands.*

TYNDALE. How long a bloody time?

ANDREWES. Queen Mary died in the sixth year of her reign. She was succeeded by her sister, Queen Elizabeth.

TYNDALE. Who was also not of the 'reform persuasion'?

ANDREWES. The Queen was certainly a Protestant in doctrine. No holy relics, miracles or pilgrimages. Nor purgatory. Priests may marry. But there are still priests.

TYNDALE. And bishops.

ANDREWES. Some said reform should go further. Some that it had gone far enough.

TYNDALE (*the chapel*). To this.

ANDREWES. But also this.

ANDREWES *hands him the folio. He himself opens* TYNDALE*'s Pentateuch.*

TYNDALE. Set out in verses.

ANDREWES. But, nonetheless.

TYNDALE (*reading*). 'In the beginning God created the Heaven and the Earth. And the Earth was without form and void, and darkness was upon the deep.'

ANDREWES. Ah. You have 'void and empty'.

TYNDALE. 'And the spirit of God – '

ANDREWES *and* TYNDALE. ' – moved upon the water.'

ANDREWES. I would find a word for God's reflection on the waters and the Earth as he made them in the image of his beauty. Like a glass?

TYNDALE (*turning pages*). 'Pane' means 'surface'.

ANDREWES (*so-so*). 'Surface.'

TYNDALE (*reading*). 'And the serpent said unto the woman: "Ye shall not surely die." '

ANDREWES. And in yours?

TYNDALE. 'Tush ye shall not die.'

ANDREWES. Indeed. And yet, / you will observe –

TYNDALE (*at Genesis 6:4*). 'And there were *giants* in the Earth in those days'?

ANDREWES. Yes?

TYNDALE. '*Nephilim.*' The word means 'tyrants'.

ANDREWES. The King is unhappy with any reference to tyrants.

TYNDALE (*who has reached Genesis 38:27–8*). 'And it came to pass in the time of her travail... And it came to pass when she travailed... And it came to pass...'

ANDREWES. And you rendered it...

TYNDALE. With more variety.

ANDREWES. But perhaps, less majesty?

TYNDALE. 'When time was come'?

ANDREWES. It's... simple.

TYNDALE. Clear.

Slight pause. ANDREWES *finds the Gospels.*

But, 'to make that better which your predecessors left / so good...'

ANDREWES. But you might wish to see the Gospels.

He hands the new Gospels to TYNDALE, *who opens them.*

For an instance, Matthew 5.

As TYNDALE *finds the chapter and* ANDREWES *finds Tyndale's New Testament:*

(*Quotes.*) 'And his disciples came to him, and he opened his mouth and taught them, saying...'

TYNDALE (*from memory*). '... Blessed are the poor in spirit...'

ANDREWES. '... for theirs is the Kingdom of Heaven.'

Pause.

TYNDALE. 'Blessed are they that mourn…'?

As ANDREWES *reads out Tyndale's Beatitudes from Matthew 5,* TYNDALE *finds them in the new version:*

ANDREWES. '… for they shall be comforted.'

TYNDALE. 'Blessed are the meek…'?

ANDREWES. '… for they shall inherit the earth.'

TYNDALE. 'Blessed are they which hunger and thirst after righteousness…'

ANDREWES. '… for they shall be filled.'

TYNDALE. 'Blessed are the merciful…'

ANDREWES. '… for they shall obtain mercy.'

TYNDALE. 'Blessed are the pure in heart: for they shall see God.'

ANDREWES. 'Blessed are the peacemakers…'

TYNDALE. '… for they shall be called the children of God.'

ANDREWES. 'Blessed are they which suffer persecution for righteousness' sake: for theirs is the Kingdom of Heaven. Blessed are ye, when men revile you, and persecute you, and shall falsely say all manner of evil sayings against you for my sake. Rejoice, and be glad, for great is your reward in Heaven.'

TYNDALE. You have 'exceeding glad'.

ANDREWES. But otherwise?

TYNDALE. The same.

ANDREWES. Verily, I say unto you.

He goes to Revelation 21:1-3.

From Matthew unto Revelation. From the first book to the last.

ANDREWES *reads from Tyndale's New Testament.*

'And I saw a new Heaven and a new Earth. For the first Heaven, and the first Earth, were vanished away; and there was no more sea.'

Pause. He holds up Tyndale's testament.

If you have come to count your fruit, you have but to raise your hand up to the tree and pick it.

Pause. TYNDALE *turns the pages of the Gospels, seeing his words. Then, reaching Matthew 16:18, he sees something else.*

TYNDALE. And yet… 'Thou art Peter and upon this rock… I will build my "church".'

Slight pause.

ANDREWES. Yes.

TYNDALE *finds a passage in 1 Corinthians 13.*

TYNDALE. And… 'Though I speak with tongues of men and angels, and yet have no "charity", I were even as sounding brass, or a tinkling cymbal.'

ANDREWES. What, you have 'spake' for 'speak'?

TYNDALE. And 'love' for 'charity'.

ANDREWES *says nothing.*

And priests and bishops? 'Penance' and 'confession'?

ANDREWES. These are matters of dispute between us.

TYNDALE. There are still matters of dispute?

ANDREWES. Evidently.

He shows TYNDALE *the list.*

TYNDALE. This is the cause of your deputation?

ANDREWES. Yes. In fact, my fellows may yet be returned –

TYNDALE (*the list*). Mark 52 'verse 10'?

ANDREWES. Some say 'thy faith hath saved thee', some 'thy faith hath healed thee'.

TYNDALE. What, salvation a task for the physician?

ANDREWES. Yes, for in the Greek…

TYNDALE. And the second Kings, chapter twenty-two?

ANDREWES. Is the story of the boy-king Josiah. Who defiled the high altars and broke the images in pieces.

TYNDALE. And the contention?

ANDREWES. Some contend it should not be defiling 'altars' but 'high places'. And not breaking images, but merely 'idols'.

TYNDALE (*looking at* ANDREWES*'s altar*). For 'there are some as say it should go further, and some who say it has gone far enough'.

ANDREWES. Yes, as I say.

TYNDALE. Oh, verily. 'Verily, I say unto you.'

ANDREWES. This is, what, Matthew?

TYNDALE. When you say 'truly', 'clearly', 'evidently'. And 'the breadth thereof' when you would – clearly – say 'its breadth', as you say 'its author'? Why translate into an ancient tongue?

ANDREWES. What, you would have us novelists, and ape the blabber of the town?

TYNDALE. (*flipping through the new Bible, finding Titus 2:10*). So our Lord speaks as no man ever spoke out loud. Not 'picking' but 'purloining'. 'Not 'faithfulness', 'fidelity'. (*To Revelation 21:4.*) And for 'the old things are gone', 'the former things are passed away'. To sacrifice the clear to the majestic.

ANDREWES. No, to make the majestic clear.

TYNDALE. To smooth out the rough and rugged places. To sacrifice the meaning to the music. To render chapters into verses, like a register. And for all the 'blesseds' and the 'holies' and the small still voice, you have sucked the sweet pith from my work and spat it out.

ANDREWES. No man spits you out.

TYNDALE. And to what end?

ANDREWES. There is no end.

TYNDALE. Oh no? Not to turn back time? To snatch God's word from the hands of seamstresses and ploughboys and hand it back to Bishops? Not 'no further' but 'too far'?

ANDREWES. I have said. There is no restoring of popish doctrine.

TYNDALE (*grabbing the chalice and thrusting it at* ANDREWES). But of popish practice.

ANDREWES (*taking the chalice*). Men still yearn for ceremony in the Church.

TYNDALE. Evidently. And when I was a child, I spoke, understood, imagined as a child. But when I became a man –

ANDREWES. So every man, alone, upon his own fancy, is trusted to unlock the meaning of the / Scripture?

TYNDALE. Yes! If it is in a language he may understand. So, shall we to work?

TYNDALE *pulls the cloths off the table. The candlesticks, basin and cross clatter across the floor. He drags the table into the centre of the chapel.*

Do you have pen and ink?

ANDREWES. Yes, I...

ANDREWES *puts down the chalice.* TYNDALE *puts the Bibles, the new version and the list on the table.*

TYNDALE. So that what was won then by the good and godly shall stay won. That the images shall yet stay broken and the altars low. That the travail and the torment of the martyrs shall not be in vain.

ANDREWES *finds the pen and ink and puts them on the altar. His hands are shaking.*

ANDREWES. I take them not in vain.

TYNDALE. Then you will be the secretary?

TYNDALE *tears the paper, handing a blank piece to* ANDREWES *to note down the decisions. He looks up the first text on the list.*

Romans 10:10... 'For with the heart men believeth' should be 'for the belief of the heart justifieth'.

ANDREWES (*writing*). If you so will it.

TYNDALE. 'Confession' shall be 'knowledge'.

ANDREWES. If it is your wish.

TYNDALE. 2 Thessalonians?

ANDREWES (*from memory*). 'Brethren stand fast and... hold to? the traditions which ye have been taught.'

TYNDALE. So, 'Keep the ordinances which ye have learnt.'
2 Samuel –

ANDREWES. But surely there are texts on which we might find a
via media. Faith 'saving' or faith 'healing'. Might we not say,
'thy faith hath made thee whole?'

TYNDALE. This is but patching.

ANDREWES. It is compromise.

TYNDALE. Then you may have your 'whole' if I may have my
'learn'.

ANDREWES. So be it.

TYNDALE. And in John, one flock.

ANDREWES. Yes?

TYNDALE. And 'love' not 'charity'. Not 'penance' but
'repetance'. Not 'church', but 'congregation'. (*Finding a text.*)
And – Ephesians 6:12?

He goes to the folio and finds it.

ANDREWES. 'For we wrestle…'

TYNDALE. 'For we wrestle not against flesh and blood, but
against… (*Finding the text.*) the rulers of the darkness of the
world.' And what are they?

ANDREWES. The phrase implies satanic forces –

TYNDALE. But it means 'worldly rulers'…

ANDREWES (*writing 'worldly rulers' down*). Paul instructs – in
your translation – every man to submit himself to the powers
that be.

TYNDALE. Yet does not Peter say: 'We ought more to obey God
than man'?

ANDREWES. You say in your book the tyrant is a scourge by
which God chastises us. And it is therefore thankful that we are
subjected to him.

TYNDALE. When I wrote that I was yet alive. Should they that
burn God's Word – God's subjects – be set above God's law?
That law which you forswear for 'the lure of base desire and
flattery'? And which only love and mercy comprehend?

ANDREWES. 'For the man that has not that written on his heart shall never truly come to Christ, no, though all the angels were to teach him.'

Pause.

TYNDALE. So what is your heart's plague, Lord Bishop?

ANDREWES. I had thought it… to be damsons.

Pause.

But I fear it is that I am such a man. And that you are come, that I might know.

TYNDALE shows ANDREWES a prison cell. We see the CLERK, six years older then when we last saw him, thin and pale, and the CHAPLAIN, who is of course the young ANDREWES. The CHAPLAIN has a lit candle.

CLERK. Master Chaplain.

CHAPLAIN. Master Clerk.

CLERK. You are past your time.

CHAPLAIN. Yet the time we have will be sufficient for our business.

CLERK. You are here to save my soul.

CHAPLAIN. And your body if you will it.

CLERK. Should you 'reduce me to conformity'.

CHAPLAIN. Should you abjure your false, unlawful and felonious positions.

The CLERK puts his hand out.

You will shake my hand?

Slight pause.

CLERK. What positions?

CHAPLAIN. First, that you are a schismatic.

CLERK. I deny this. I seek but a fellowship and communion of the faithful, pure of papistry and heresy.

CHAPLAIN. Then second, that you are a slanderer, in that you defame the Church.

CLERK. Only when its ministration is idolatrous.

CHAPLAIN. And third that you are traitor to Her Majesty.

CLERK. How am I so?

CHAPLAIN. By slandering the Church of which she is the head.

CLERK. I say that its reformation should proceed without tarrying for worldly rulers.

CHAPLAIN. You will subvert the state if you cannot form it to your fancy?

CLERK. I have no interest in the state.

CHAPLAIN. Yet you would hold all in common?

CLERK. I would live as the apostles.

CHAPLAIN. Yet you call the Church a heresy?

The CLERK *thrusts a Bible at the* CHAPLAIN.

CLERK. Where is baptism of infants? Where are fasting days and Lent? Where is kneeling? Where are images? Where patronage?

CHAPLAIN. And if a fellow of your congregation kneels to pray or fasts on Friday? He is an heretic?

CLERK. It is not possible.

CHAPLAIN. And happy is that case. For does not our Saviour say that if 'thy right hand offend thee, cut it off'? For it is profitable that one man perish, to protect the whole?

Slight pause.

So you would visit upon him what is here visited on you.

The CHAPLAIN *turns to go.*

CLERK. Master Andrewes.

CHAPLAIN. Yes?

CLERK. It is no matter.

CHAPLAIN. Then so be it.

CLERK. I am here in chains for three years. I am kept from healthful exercise. In the winter it is cold and the evenings dark. Sir, I pray you...

CHAPLAIN. Ah, Master Clerk. In this you are most happy. The solitary and contemplative life I hold most blessed. Yours is the life that I should choose.

He turns again.

CLERK. My life? My life is over.

CHAPLAIN. Yes.

CLERK. Whilst you are the Queen's chaplain.

CHAPLAIN. Yes.

CLERK. Did you betray me?

CHAPLAIN. You betrayed yourself.

The CHAPLAIN *blows out the candle. He and the* CLERK *disappear.* TYNDALE *has gone.* ANDREWES *is still. Now he lowers his head and spreads his arms out across the altar table.*

ANDREWES. O base and loathsome sinner that I am.

WARD *is the first of the translators to have entered the chapel. He has his escritoire.*

WARD. My lord?

ANDREWES *stands and turns to the entering* SAVILLE, ABBOT, CHADERTON *and* OVERALL. *They are bemused by the remaining mess on the floor.*

SAVILLE. My lord, you will forgive us. This is the second time we are gathered for our conference.

ABBOT. Though we are pleased to see you at our work.

Pause.

WARD. Have you consid-dered the proposals for the t-t-texts, my lord?

ANDREWES. Yes. Yes, I... (*With a vague gesture at the detritus.*) I have been at heavy labour.

SAVILLE. Clearly, my lord.

Pause.

ABBOT. So might you, bring forth...

ANDREWES. Masters, I own myself surprised by your petition. I am but one of fifty-four...

OVERALL (*sotto voce, to* ANDREWES). Lord Bishop...

Impatience as WARD *sees the list that* ANDREWES *has written, on the table, and hurries to it.*

CHADERTON. My lord, to say that you are one of fifty-four is to say our Lord was one of three and ten.

WARD. Are those the changes?

As WARD *scans the list,* ANDREWES *hurries back to rescue it:*

'Ordinance.' 'Flock.' 'Love.'

OVERALL. 'Flock'?

ANDREWES. It is but scribbling –

Affecting to reach for the list, ANDREWES *knocks over the inkwell, pouring ink on to the paper.*

CHADERTON. Ah...

ANDREWES. I...

Attempting to rescue the list, he makes the blotting worse. The ink gets over his hands.

I fear I...

ABBOT. Is there a blotter?

WARD. It seems not. (*From memory, as* SAVILLE *finds a altar napkin.*) Nonetheless, my Lord Bishop would strike out 'penance'.

OVERALL. Would he?

WARD. As we wrestle not with d-d-darkness but with 'worldly rulers'.

ABBOT (*surprised*). In what, Ephesians 6?

OVERALL. Ephesians 6 is in contention?

WARD *is finding the text so he knows the chapter and verse.*

SAVILLE (*the napkin*). Not intended for so humble an employment.

CHADERTON. Is aught else clear?

WARD holds up the inky paper.

SAVILLE. But surely, my lord, you can remember…

ABBOT. Perhaps another copy might be made.

CHADERTON. It is clear enough which way my lord is facing.

ABBOT. Archbishop Bancroft is most urgent in this business.

OVERALL. Then let us not displease him with its outcome.

ANDREWES (*waving his still inky hand*). Might someone fetch some water?

A moment. WARD, as the most junior, accepts this is his task. He turns to the door to see that SIR JOHN HARINGTON, eighteen, has entered through it, followed by HENRY, Prince of Wales, sixteen, the ten-year-old CHARLES, Duke of York, his chaperone LADY ALLETTA CAREY and the thirty-five-year-old WILLIAM LAUD. The ROYAL PARTY are a blaze of colour. They see a group of dark DIVINES, much exercised, huddled round an inky paper.

HARINGTON. Room, room, for His Highness Prince of Wales. Room for His Grace the Duke of York. All be uncovered! Make room, make room!

The CLERICS move as quickly as they can to take off their hats and fall to their knees.

HENRY. My lords. Pray you to be upstanding. I am not my father.

Those who have got to their knees rise. All bow.

And please you to be covered.

As the CLERICS put on their hats, the ROYAL PARTY takes in the scene, including the books on the altar and its furniture on the floor. Unexpectedly, LAUD walks forward and bows elaborately to the altar.

HARINGTON. Master Laud?

LAUD. Is not this Christ's table?

ABBOT (*who knows LAUD and doesn't like him*). Hmph.

HENRY. My lords, forgive us for this interruption. We are returning from the hunt at Theobalds. Sir John Harington is my companion. This is my Lady Carey, companion to my brother. The Duke of York.

The CLERICS *bow to* CHARLES.

HENRY. And... Master Laud of St John's College Cambridge.

ANDREWES *and* ABBOT *know this to be wrong.*

LAUD. St John's Oxford, sir. And I am chaplain to my Lord of Lichfield.

A note of embarrassment at LAUD *making this pedantic point. He takes this as requiring a supplement.*

And have preached before your father.

ABBOT. Once.

HENRY. We are here on the commission of my father. Who knows of your deliberations on the matter of his Bible and is sharp to learn that all dispute is happily resolved.

The CLERICS *look at each other and the table and the inky paper.*

CHARLES. Before Archbishop Bancroft dies.

A difficult pause.

HENRY. We will all die, Charles.

CHARLES *realises he's committed a faux pas. Suddenly, to lighten the atmosphere,* HENRY *grabs* OVERALL*'s cap and plonks it on* CHARLES*'s head.*

Maybe I will make you my Archbishop. With great skirts to hide your legs. What say you, London? Ely?

CHARLES *is upset.* LADY CAREY *takes the cap from his head and gives it back to* HENRY.

LADY CAREY (*reproving*). Your Highness.

HENRY *smiles, and tosses the cap back to* OVERALL.

HENRY. So what is going on? There has clearly been much swordplay here.

SAVILLE. Sir, we are gathered to hear the adjudication of my Lord of Ely on the few remaining matters of controversy.

HENRY. My Lord of Ely is a man of learning, gravity and wisdom. Is this the list?

WARD gives HENRY the original list of disputed texts.

WARD. In fact, my Lord of Ely has already judged the most p-p-pressing questions of controversy between us.

HENRY. A veritable Solomon.

ANDREWES. But nonetheless...

HENRY. My lord?

ANDREWES. There is a wealth of learning here assembled. Why should all follow one man's fancy? If we are to return our workings to the anvil, why should we bring but one hammer to the task?

OVERALL. After all, it is possible for the most learned men to alter their opinions.

ABBOT. Even so.

OVERALL. We have among our company one that teaches how both Earth and Sun are at the centre of the universe.

HENRY looks rounds quizzically, SAVILLE is forced to acknowledge.

HENRY. Well, if Sir Henry will not cast his ballot for or against Copernicus, then at least we can insist he raise his hand for 'penance' or 'repentance'.

Slight pause.

SAVILLE. In the Greek, '*metanoeo*' means 'to turn in heart and mind'.

WARD opens his escritoire and finds another piece of paper, on which he notes down the decisions. During this, CHARLES goes and looks through the various Bible texts strewn about the chapel.

HENRY. Then, repentence. And 'confession' or 'acknowledge'? (*To CHADERTON.*) Master...

CHADERTON. 'Acknowledge', certainly.

HENRY. Who concurs?

CHADERTON, WARD, ABBOT and SAVILLE raise their hands. LAUD mouths 'rules' to OVERALL.

And so, what else?

OVERALL. Your Highness, the Archbishop in his wisdom laid down certain rules for the translation, with regard to ancient usages like priest and church and charity.

HENRY. I know. I was present at the conference. I was as old then as Charles is now.

Slight pause.

Who is for following the Archbishop in these ancient rules?

ABBOT and OVERALL put their hands up, SAVILLE about to.

Or rather, for striking out anew?

CHADERTON, WARD and then SAVILLE vote.

CHADERTON. So might we say 'ordinances' rather than 'traditions'?

WARD. 'Flock' not 'fold'.

HENRY looks round. SAVILLE and ABBOT aquiesce. HENRY hands the list to WARD.

OVERALL. This will not be to the Archbishop's liking.

HENRY. Yet it is to mine.

OVERALL. And then there is Ephesians 6.

LAUD. The beginning of that chapter enjoins children to obey their parents.

HARINGTON. There'll be no revision there.

Laughter. CHARLES joins in. He has a folio of the new Bible in his hands.

OVERALL. Where we wrestle not with flesh and blood, but against 'the rulers of the darkness of this world'.

ABBOT. It is a figure, sir. The rulers are not earthly beings. It means the Devil.

OVERALL. Yet was it not writ 'worldly rulers'?

Difficult pause.

HENRY. Writ by whom?

OVERALL *shrugs. Pause.*

CHADERTON (*rescue attempt*). And yet, is not the Pope of Rome a worldly ruler? And the Emperor? And the perfidious Royal House of Spain?

ABBOT. Perfidious and hostile.

OVERALL. Yet is it not to our King's liking that his princely son be married to the Infanta?

HENRY. It is not to mine.

Slight pause.

As it is not to my or any true godly Christian's liking that Europe in its southern and its western parts shall remain in thrall to popery. To my liking or intent.

WARD. A new Josiah!

HENRY *demurs at this hyperbole.*

HENRY (*turning to go*). And now that this / is settled –

CHARLES (*with the new text*). My lords, how is this done?

ABBOT. In – what respect, Lord Duke?

CHARLES. How is the translation wrought?

Slight pause.

SAVILLE. Why, by old men sitting in a circle, with many books before them. And one man reads out the text – from one of these books, the Bishops' Bible – and the others speak out when they wish so to amend it.

CHARLES. Show me.

LADY CAREY. Your Grace, we are due at / Hampton Court...

CHARLES *hands the folio to* SAVILLE.

CHARLES. Show me.

SAVILLE *takes the book.*

Isaiah, chapter two, verse four. 'And they shall break...'

The CLERICS *take other copies of the Bible:* WARD *Matthew,* ABBOT *Geneva,* OVERALL *Coverdale and* CHADERTON *the Hebrew text.* WARD *notes.*

SAVILLE. 'And they shall break their swords also into mattocks, and their spears to make scythes.'

    WARD *catches up.*

ABBOT. Mattocks?

WARD. Matthew's has 'swords and spears to make scythes and saws thereof'.

OVERALL. And Coverdale adds 'sickles'.

SAVILLE. Adds?

OVERALL (*emphasising the crowding of sibilants*). 'So that they shall break their swords and spears, to make scythes, sickles and saws thereof.'

    Clearly too much alliteration.

ABBOT. Swords into mattocks and spears into – 'millstones'?

CHADERTON. Or why not, '*mazmeroth*', into 'hooks'.

OVERALL. Then swords to – 'hayrakes'?

CHADERTON. '*Itim*.' (*To* ANDREWES.) Plowbeams?

ANDREWES. Plowshares.

ABBOT. 'Swords into plowshares.'

SAVILLE. And so, 'spears'?

WARD (*to* ANDREWES). My lord?

ANDREWES. 'Spears into – pruning hooks.'

    Agreed.

SAVILLE. 'And one people shall not lift up a weapon against another. Neither shall they learn to fight from – henceforth.'

ABBOT. 'Nation shall not lift up a sword against nation.'

CHARLES. 'Neither shall they fight any more'?

    The DIVINES *approve and maybe applaud.*

It is the passage most of all to the liking of my father. He too is like a Solomon.

LADY CAREY. *Rex pacificus.*

Alarm.

CHADERTON. But surely, Lord Duke… the papist threat…

OVERALL. Hmph.

CHARLES. I was born lame. The doctors would have me put in iron leggings. My Lady Carey had me made high riding boots of Spanish leather. Strong, but yet supple.

He puts out his leg and twists it, to demonstrate that he is no longer disabled. A round of applause.

Were I your Archbishop, brother, I would counsel you to be supple too. Even with the Spanish and the Pope.

HENRY. So we are decided?

WARD. All is noted down.

HENRY (*to* ANDREWES). Yet I wonder, Lord of Ely, at your silence.

ANDREWES. As I said, in the presence of such learning, is there want of my opinion?

Slight pause.

OVERALL. '*Aqua lavit manus coram populo.*'

Pause.

LADY CAREY. Lord Duke?

CHARLES. It's Pontius Pilate. When he washed his hands in front of all the people.

Slight pause.

HENRY. Who knows, but that the Church's future rule may hang upon this resolution. Lords, fare you well.

The CLERICS *bow,* HENRY *goes out followed by* HARINGTON, CHARLES *and* LADY CAREY. WARD *stands, collecting his new notes, eager to deliver them to the revisers.*

CHADERTON. Certainly a new Josiah.

WARD. My lord, may we set out at once?

ANDREWES *aquiesces.*

Shall we're b-b-bear this news together, Master Chaderton?

OVERALL. Bear it where?

WARD. To the St-t-tationers' Hall.

CHADERTON. With all Godspeed. Good day, my lords.

CHADERTON *goes out.*

WARD (*to* ANDREWES). You are content, my lord?

ANDREWES. Evidently.

WARD *goes quickly out, with his notes, but leaving his escritoire and the Isaiah changes behind.*

SAVILLE. Master Laud, do you not stay with the Royal Party?

LAUD. The Prince of Wales is set for Richmond, and the Duke to Hampton Court.

SAVILLE. And you for…

LAUD. Kent, where I hold a living.

ABBOT. Do you now.

LAUD (*to* ABBOT). You will be content with this, my lord?

ABBOT. To a degree.

OVERALL. What, with 'elders' and with 'congregation'?

ABBOT *is a little so concerned, but doesn't want to say so in front of* OVERALL *and* LAUD.

ABBOT. The Church will stand. And such as men call puritans did never differ from the rest on any point of substance. But about circumstance, and ceremony.

OVERALL *looks witheringly at* ABBOT.

On doctrine – *sola scriptura, sola fides* – we are at one.

SAVILLE (*the new Bible*). Thus far but no further, Master Dean.

OVERALL. You think so? I'd say, that all depends on who steps out to Canterbury.

This is a statement too far.

ABBOT. I am stayed for at Westminster.

He puts his hand out to ANDREWES.

Lord Bishop.

ANDREWES *shakes his hand.*

Sir Henry?

SAVILLE. Yes. My lord.

ABBOT *throws a grimy glance at* OVERALL *as he and* SAVILLE *go, leaving* ANDREWES *with* OVERALL *and* LAUD.

OVERALL (*angry*). My lord, I am with Prince Henry.

ANDREWES. How so?

OVERALL. I too marvel at your silence.

ANDREWES. Why should I speak, when so many are so eloquent?

OVERALL. I cannot believe you to / be blithe –

ANDREWES (*seeing the transcription*). Ah, the changes in Isaiah.

He picks up the paper.

(*To* OVERALL.) Might you catch up, Master Ward? And send the maid in, with some water, as you go?

ANDREWES *hands the paper to* OVERALL, *who is aware he is being dismissed.*

Perhaps it should be 'neither shall they learn war any more'.

OVERALL. It is certainly – the more majestical.

OVERALL *goes out.*

LAUD. My lord, I too wonder at your actions.

ANDREWES *looks questioningly at* LAUD.

On the Church and priests, had you made your throw, the dice would have fallen even.

ANDREWES. Then perhaps it is well I did not do so.

LAUD. Some might see it as a pretty calculation, for London's preference to be known, and Ely's not.

ANDREWES. Master Laud, I am no reckoner.

LAUD. But perhaps you ought to be.

ANDREWES. The Archbishop may yet defy the augury of his physicians.

LAUD. Tush.

ANDREWES. Bishop Abbot voted for the Church.

LAUD. And spoke against confession, penance and tradition. And for wrestling with earthly rulers.

ANDREWES. Oh, Master Laud. Perhaps he fears with me that if we turn back time, we render all their travail and their torment vain.

LAUD. Whose torment?

ANDREWES *picks up Tyndale and Matthew's Bibles.*

My lord, we live in different times.

ANDREWES. Certainly we shall not die for what we do.

Enter MARY, *with a basin of water and a towel.*

LAUD. Then, would I have you live, to preserve your Church.

ANDREWES. How so?

MARY. My lord, your water.

ANDREWES. Thank you.

MARY *puts the basin and towel in front of him.*

LAUD (*gesturing at the altar cloth on the floor*). And might she not…?

ANDREWES *gestures to* MARY *to tidy up.*

ANDREWES. And light the candle.

MARY *tidies the room and the altar table, putting back the candles and lighting one, as –*

(*To* LAUD.) So, Master Laud, what would you have us do?

LAUD. Unstitch the cope, but keep the surplice. Melt down the censors, but rub up the chalices. Unthrone the Pope, but not the bishops. Nor the King. Dismantle purgatory, but keep tradition, sacraments, good works, and majesty.

Slight pause.

ANDREWES. Master Laud. You are a glass in which I see myself.

LAUD. Then see a man that sits upon a throne at Canterbury.

Pause.

ANDREWES. It is... not an honour I had looked for.

LAUD. Tush again.

ANDREWES. Bishop Abbot is a fit and worthy / candidate –

LAUD. Bishop Abbot is a puritan.

ANDREWES. The Scots would not look kindly on me.

LAUD. There is but one Scot whose opinion counts in this. And but one Englishman.

ANDREWES. You mean, that the King embraces / both within his person?

LAUD. I mean that he will talk to the Archbishop.

ANDREWES. Yes, I have no doubt.

LAUD. So write to him.

ANDREWES. The King?

LAUD. No, the Archbishop. (*To* MARY.) Is there a pen and ink?

> MARY *gets* WARD*'s escritoire and brings it to* ANDREWES. *He looks at his hands, which are shaking.*

And call the Bishop's secretary.

MARY (*to* ANDREWES). I can write, my lord.

> ANDREWES *and* LAUD *look at her, in a little surprise.*

ANDREWES. Then... very well.

Slight pause.

LAUD. Lord Bishop, I am mindful of the future.

ANDREWES. Tomorrow is a glass in which no man can look with certainty.

LAUD. Except that he looks there to determine what to do today.

LAUD gestures towards MARY, *waiting to take his dictation.*

To draw a line marked 'thus far, but no further'.

He gestures to the folios.

And for this book to be that line. This book, as it was before today.

Slight pause.

Lest the fond and foolish misreader of the word saw off the branch on which he sits.

ANDREWES. Ah, Master Laud. I am with the young Prince. I would that there were no more fighting.

LAUD. I too. But like you, my lord, I fear that if we are to keep the Church as you and I would wish it, free from schismatism, treachery and slander, then perhaps the supple leather may not suffice to keep us straight. Might not we need the iron leggings too?

Slight pause.

Or else, what may befall archbishops, priests and majesties?

LAUD gives a slight bow, and goes out. ANDREWES *breathes deeply, looks at his inky hands.*

MARY. Sir, I am ready. If you wish it.

Pause.

ANDREWES. Yes. 'To Richard Cantuar.' That's C – a – n – t – u – a – r.

MARY. Is that his name?

ANDREWES. It is the Latin name for Canterbury.

As ANDREWES *dictates, he washes his hands.*

'Your Grace, my most humble salutation, and my most fervent wishes for… My most humble salutation.'

He checks.

Did you write that?

MARY. Yes, my lord.

ANDREWES. 'Today I was visited by a deputation of translators.'

MARY. '...translators.' Yes, my lord.

ANDREWES. 'As you may surmise, there was much zeal and hot controversy in our conference.'

MARY. 'Zeal' has a 'zed', my lord?

ANDREWES. It does. But strike that sentence out. (*Dictating.*) 'It is possible that some amendments were made in undue haste.'

MARY (*as she writes*). These are amendments to the translation, sir?

ANDREWES. Indeed. 'It is possible you might wish to revise them.'

MARY (*as she writes*). That means, change what you have decided here?

ANDREWES. Yes, surely. Notably in the Epistles, Matthew, John, the Acts – do I go too fast?

MARY. A little, sir.

ANDREWES. 'Matthew, John, Acts, second Kings.'

MARY (*as she writes*). You would alter Matthew, John and Kings?

ANDREWES. 'The other changes I see as indifferent.'

MARY (*as she writes*). That's the other changes to the meaning of the Bible, sir?

ANDREWES. Evidently. 'I remain your faithful servant, and your friend.'

MARY (*as she writes*). For fear that otherwise they might be read by the fond and foolish?

ANDREWES. So, is it written?

MARY. 'And your friend.' Yes, sir.

She hands the letter to him.

ANDREWES. Your hand is fair.

MARY. My father taught me.

ANDREWES. Then you owe him much.

MARY. And to read God's Word.

ANDREWES. For that gift, even more.

MARY. And that the Word of God is for all time.

ANDREWES. And so it is. But his crooked and imperfect creature, man, is not of all time, and it is to him that these words speak.

MARY. So to preserve 'tradition, works and majesty'.

ANDREWES. Indeed.

MARY. But do not Christians wrestle with the rulers of this world? And that justly? So that the time that is for all time comes. And that full speedily?

ANDREWES. What, in Heaven?

MARY. No, on Earth.

ANDREWES. You wish for heavenly perfection here on Earth?

MARY. Was it not so once, back in the garden?

ANDREWES. Before the fall.

MARY. And in St John's dreaming of the great apocalypse in Revelation?

ANDREWES. As you say, his dream.

She picks up the folios of the new Bible and puts them on the altar table.

MARY. And in your Bible, will the Apostles on the day of Pentecost yet part all their possessions, and see visions and dream dreams?

ANDREWES. But for a time, and in a time.

MARY. And is Josiah yet eight years old when he begins his reign of thirty and one years in Jerusalem?

ANDREWES. Yes...

MARY. And does he still put down the idolators, and break down the houses of the sodomites, and bring forth all the priests out of the cities? And sacrifice the priests on their high altars, and break their images in pieces?

ANDREWES. Yet have we not had a sufficiency of / sacrifice –

MARY. And does John still promise us new Heaven and new Earth? And what right has any man to say there is sufficiency of dreaming? What right to say, 'Come now, we have gone far enough'?

She takes the letter to the candle.

ANDREWES. Yet if there is but God's Word / and men's mind, then what –

MARY. Sir, may I burn this letter? May I burn it now.

ANDREWES. No, unless you would be cast out from / my household.

She moves her other hand towards the candle.

MARY. Or would you I burn my / hand –

ANDREWES. No, please. No.

He holds out his hand. A moment. She gives him the letter. He scrawls a postscript. He hands it back to MARY. *She looks at it.*

MARY *(reading)*. 'Forgive my hand. Your successor should be Bishop Abbot.' And your name.

Slight pause.

Why, sir?

ANDREWES. You ask me why?

MARY. Yes, sir.

ANDREWES. Then, because… I knew a man who would not spend his remaining earthly days at breaking windows.

MARY. So you would scrawl across God's Word to save a window?

ANDREWES. No, but I would not spend my remaining days at breaking bones. In visitation to such men, and women, in their prisons, on their gallows, at the stake. Brave as they are. Right as they claim themselves to be, today, tomorrow, and for ever. So, I will not seek elevation. I will stay here, in this place, beneath these windows, with the beauty of these words, which John tells us were from the beginning. For I would see darkly, Mary.

MARY. Darkly, sir?

ANDREWES. I would not see the fate of kings and princes. Nor my fate, nor yours. Fearing that one day you will strip and smash and burn such places as this place once more.

A moment.

Will you take the letter? Will you do as I have told you?

MARY. Yes, my lord.

They look at each other.

ANDREWES. For now.

MARY *goes.* ANDREWES *looks round his chapel.*

'And darkness was upon the deep.'

A thought strikes him. He goes to the Hebrew Bible and opens it.

'*Al pane teham.*' '*Al pane hannayyie.*' Not surface. Are you still there?

TYNDALE *is there.*

TYNDALE. Try Coverdale.

ANDREWES *finds Coverdale's Great Bible.*

ANDREWES. 'And darkness was upon the face of the deep, and the spirit of God moved', again, 'upon the face of the waters'.

Pause.

The sea a glass in which we see God's face.

TYNDALE. God's face a glass in which man sees himself.

Slight pause. ANDREWES *puts his hand on the folios.*

ANDREWES. The ploughboy reads the book.

TYNDALE. And sees God face to face.

ANDREWES. And knows…?

TYNDALE. … as he is known.

Slight pause.

ANDREWES. I would not so see him.

TYNDALE. Yet – I am still here.

TYNDALE *puts his hand on the folios. Blackout.*
End of play.

The Making of the English Bible 1382–1611

1382	During the reign of Richard II, the first Wyclif Bible is translated from Latin into English. It is condemned by the Synod of Blackfriars.
1401	Henry IV bans Wyclif's teachings and books, and makes heresy a burning offence.
1408	The Constitutions of Oxford declare translating Scripture or reading the English Bible to be heretical.
1414	A revolt by Wyclif's Lollard followers, led by Sir John Oldcastle, is put down by Henry V.
1428	At the order of Pope Martin V, John Wyclif's body is exhumed, cut up, burnt and thrown into the River Swift at Lutterworth.
1440	Johannes Gutenburg invents the mechanical movable-type printing press.
1509	Henry VIII comes to the throne.
1521	Henry VIII attacks the teachings of Martin Luther and defends the seven sacraments of the church.
1524	William Tyndale flees England for northern Europe, in order to translate and print a Bible translated from the original tongues.
1526	Translated from the Greek, Tyndale's New Testament is printed in Germany and smuggled into England, to be burnt in large numbers by Cardinal Wolsey.
1529	Cardinal Wolsey falls from power. Sir Thomas More becomes Chancellor, campaigns against heretics and attacks Tyndale and his writings.
1530	Translated from the Hebrew, Tyndale's Pentateuch (the first five books of the Old Testament) is published in Antwerp.
1531	Henry VIII is declared Head of the Church in England. Tyndale replies to More's attack.

1533	Henry VIII divorces Catherine of Aragon, marries Anne Boleyn and is excommunicated by the Pope.
1534	Archbishop Thomas Cranmer presides over a convocation which calls for an English translation of the Bible to be made.
1535	In England, Sir Thomas More is executed for treason. In Flanders, William Tyndale is arrested for heresy. Translated from Latin and German into English, Miles Coverdale's Bible is published with Henry VIII's permission.
1536	Anne Boleyn is beheaded in London and William Tyndale dies the stake in Flanders. The dissolution of the English monasteries begins, provoking the Pilgrimage of Grace, a northern rebellion against the Reformation.
1537	A conflation of Tyndale and Coverdale's translations, the Thomas Matthew Bible, is made by John Rogers and published under the King's licence.
1539	Coverdale's revision of Matthew's Bible, the Great Bible, is put into every English church.
1543	An Act for the Advancement of True Religion bans Tyndale's Bible and forbids men below the rank of merchant and women below the class of gentlewoman from reading the Bible in English.
1547	Henry VIII dies, and his nine-year-old son succeeds him as Edward VI. All restrictions on printing and reading the Bible are repealed. Images are removed from churches and the chantries closed.
1548	The Privy Council abolishes ceremonies of candles at Candlemas, ashes on Ash Wednesday, palms on Palm Sunday and use of holy bread and water.
1549	Priests are allowed to marry. Cranmer's Book of Common Prayer is published, provoking uprisings in Cornwall.
1553	After the doomed nine-day reign of Protestant Lady Jane Grey, Catherine of Aragon's Catholic daughter Mary becomes Queen.

1555	Bible translator John Rogers is the first of nearly three hundred protestants to be burnt under Queen Mary. The Oxford martyrs Hugh Latimer, Nicholas Ridley and then Thomas Cranmer follow him to the stake.
1557	All stage plays are prohibited by Mary.
1558	Queen Mary dies, and her half-sister Elizabeth succeeds her.
1559	The Act of Uniformity is passed by three votes in Parliament. Injunctions are issued for the suppression of superstition. However, clerical vestments, signing of the cross, kneeling at communion and formal prayer are retained.
1560	Translated by Protestant exiles during Mary's reign, the Geneva Bible is published.
1563	The Church of England retains the threefold ministry of bishops, priests and deacons, and the endowment of cathedrals.
1568	Archbishop Matthew Parker's Bishops' Bible is published, and subsequently placed in every English church.
1569	A Catholic rising in Northern England is suppressed.
1570	Pope Pius V excommunicates Queen Elizabeth, and calls on Catholics to overthrow her.
1571	The thirty-nine Articles of Faith of the Church of England are sanctioned by Parliament and anti-Catholic legislation is passed.
1580	English Jesuits exiled in France mount a secret mission in England; some are arrested and executed.
1582	The Douai-Rheims translation of the New Testament is published by Catholics in France.
1583	As part of a campaign against the growth of separatist sects and puritan doctrine, the Church prohibits all preaching in private places except for the family home. Over two hundred dissident ministers are suspended.

1587	The Catholic Mary Queen of Scots is executed.
1588	The Spanish Armada is defeated.
1593	Separatists Henry Barrow and John Greenwood are executed for sedition, breaking the back of the puritan movement.
1601	Richard Bancroft, Bishop of London, offers English Catholics toleration in return for rejection of the Pope's claim to depose princes.
1603	Elizabeth I dies. James VI of Scotland is proclaimed James I of England. He repeals fines for non-attendance at church.
1604	The King convenes a religious conference at Hampton Court, at which the puritan faction is defeated. A new translation of the Bible is commissioned.
1605	The Gunpowder Plot is foiled.
1606	A new Oath of Allegiance to the English Crown is imposed, which the Pope forbids Catholics to take.
1610	Lancelot Andrewes, Bishop of Ely, defends the Oath of Allegiance in a controversy with Cardinal Bellarmine. Archbishop Richard Bancroft dies.
1611	The King James Bible is published.
1612	Two anti-trinitarian radicals are the last people to be burnt for heresy in England. Henry, Prince of Wales, dies of typhoid, leaving his brother Charles as heir to throne.
1625	James I dies and Charles I is crowned King of England. The text of the coronation sermon is 'Be thou faithful unto death.'

Afterword

Three years ago, I collaborated with the RSC in organising a conference about the King James Bible. I already knew some of its ironies: that it was commissioned as an afterthought to mollify the losing faction at a religious conference called by James I in 1604; that it was not so much a translation as a compilation of other translations, made by fifty-four scholars organised in six committees; that far from inventing modern English, it was written in a self-consciously antique style, as if a Bible today had been translated into the English of E.M. Forster or Terence Rattigan; and – in so far as its purpose was to draw a line under the English Reformation – that it was a manifest failure. But, despite all this, that it ended up being the best-selling book in the history of the world.

The conference began by comparing magnificent King James tropery with doomed contemporary attempts at revision. Examples included Ecclesiastes's 'to every thing there is a season', mangled into the 1966 Good News Bible's 'everything that happens in this world happens at the time God chooses'. In 1 Corinthians, the KJB's 'When I was a child, I spake as a child, I understood as a child, I thought as a child: but when I became a man, I put away childish things' re-emerges in the 1961 New English Bible as 'When I was a child, my speech, my outlook and my thoughts were all childish. When I grew up, I had finished with childish things', and, in the 1993 New Message Bible, as 'When I was an infant at my mother's breast, I gurgled and cooed like any infant. When I grew up, I left those infant ways for good.' For 'through a glass darkly', the New English Bible has 'puzzling reflections in a mirror', and the New Message Bible 'squinting in a fog'.

That such affronts are not unique to the twentieth century was demonstrated by David Norton in his 2011 history of the King James Bible, in which he quoted Edward Harwood's 1768 Liberal Translation of the New Testament, which instructs us to 'Survey with attention the lilies of the field, and learn from them how unbecoming it is for rational creatures to cherish a solicitous passion for gaiety and dress.'

But the main thing we did at the conference was not to praise but to demystify the 1611 text, the job the RSC likes to do to Shakespeare. The KJB was not the universal and unique Word of God, but a book made at a particular time for a particular purpose. And the scale of that purpose became clearer and clearer as the experts we brought in explained to us that the story of the English Bible is – much more than Henry VIII's dynastic and indeed romantic ambitions – the story of the English Reformation, a subject I'd never written about, and felt it was high time. Not least as the fundamentalist protestantisms of the sixteenth and seventeenth century were so eerily resonant of other religious fundamentalisms today: with their veneration of the book, their hostility to the image and suspicion of music, their sexual puritanism, their desire to unify Church and State, and their obsession with martyrdom. Even the beards.

When I started serious research for the play which arose out of the conference (along with the Bush Theatre's *Sixty-Six Books* project, which consists of responses to every book of the Bible, to which I also contributed), I realised that the half had not been told me. In particular, I discovered that the KJB was not a seven-year story but at least an eighty-six-year one, and that dozens and dozens of the coinages we think were invented by the 1611 translators came from earlier versions, from 'let there be light', 'am I my brother's keeper?', 'be fruitful and multiply', 'let my people go' and 'by the skin of my teeth', via 'tender mercies', 'a man after his own heart', 'vanity of vanities', 'sign of the times' and 'wages of sin', to 'all things to all men', 'eat, drink and be merry', 'fight the good fight', 'the powers that be' and 'grave, where is thy victory?'

The second striking realisation was that the progenitors of the King James were not comfortable clerics but – largely – outlaws. Most of the memorable Biblical phrases listed above were coined not in the hallowed cloisters of Oxford colleges nor in the sepulchral calm of the Jerusalem Chamber, but on the run. Five of the seven major English Bibles of the sixteenth century were produced in exile, and two of their makers died at the stake. Each new Bible was the manifesto of a faction in the religious wars that revolutionised Tudor England, each subsequent Bible a revision and many a riposte. If indeed the full, eighty-year-plus history of the English Bible is the story of the English Reformation, then that Bible too is spattered with blood and scorched with fire.

So, nearly sixty years before printing, one hundred and thirty years before Luther, England's John Wyclif oversaw the translation of two manuscript English Bibles from the official, fourth-century Latin Vulgate, a project which landed him in court, and led to laws which made the translation or even reading of the Bible in the vernacular a burning offence (laws under which Wyclif's own body was dug up and incinerated). Wyclif's underground Lollard followers kept alive the idea of a direct relationship between God and the individual Christian, through his Word.

Like Wyclif, the first Bible translator of the printing age saw the production of an English Bible as a matter of theology. Since Melvyn Bragg's bold decision (in his *12 Books That Changed the World*) to co-attribute the King James Bible to the first translator of the Bible from its original languages, it's been generally accepted that the 1611 version owes its greatest debt to William Tyndale. Born around 1495 in the Lollard country of the West Cotswolds, educated at Oxford, inspired by Luther, Tyndale was not a translator who became a Protestant, but a Protestant who went to great lengths to equip himself to be a translator, believing that if 'a boy that driveth the plough' had access to the Word of God in his language, he would discover how little of Catholic ritual and indeed doctrine was in there (no sacraments or relics, no bishops, popes or purgatory). Aware that Bible translation was still a capital offence, Tyndale fled England for northern Europe and spent the rest of his life trying to keep one step ahead of the imperial authorities. Betrayed by spies and corrupt collaborators, fleeing up the Rhine with the first-ever printed sheets of an English Gospel in his satchel, he nonetheless produced the first printed translations of the New Testament and the first five books of the old (the Pentateuch), which were then smuggled into England and – when found – burnt in solemn rituals by Cardinal Wolsey.

Produced under these desperate circumstances, Tyndale's New Testament nonetheless provides well over eighty per cent of the King James version. People note the sonorous musicality of the Beatitudes, but not their provenance: from 'Blessed are the poor in spirit...' all the way through to 'Blessed are ye, when men revile you...', every word but one is Tyndale's. His Old Testament coinages range from 'let there be light' and 'let my people go' to 'am I my brother's keeper', 'a man after his own heart' and 'the fat of the land'.

At the same time, Tyndale was buttressing his practice with the theory, in writings which promoted the anti-papal, Lutheran cause and provoked the ire of Catholic apologists like the heretic-burner Thomas More – the man for all seasons who kept a whipping post in his own back garden – who unjustly accused Tyndale of being a political as well as a religious revolutionary. In fact, Tyndale followed his mentor Luther (who'd been appalled by the peasant uprisings of the mid-1520s in Münster and elsewhere) in seeing kingly power as the only realistic alternative to papal infallibility. In his *The Obedience of a Christian Man*, Tyndale argues forcibly for unconditional loyalty to kings ('He that judgeth the King judgeth God and damneth God's law and ordinance'). In his play for Shakespeare's Globe, *Anne Boleyn*, Howard Brenton dramatises how Henry's second Queen alerted him to Tyndale's congenial opinions on the royal supremacy, and overtures were made for Tyndale's return to England. Sensibly (in view of Anne's fate), he refused them. However, a year after More's arrest for opposing the King's defiance of the Pope, Tyndale was lured from his Antwerp safe house by an English adventurer (possibly in More's pay) and tried by the imperial authorities for heresy. Despite a half-hearted attempt by Thomas Cromwell to secure his release, Tyndale was strangled and his body burnt at Vilvoorde in October 1536. For John Foxe, in his *Acts and Monuments of Martyrs*, Tyndale's last words were 'Lord, ope the King of England's eyes.'

The irony of Tyndale's death – of which he may or may not have been aware – is that Henry's eyes were opened already. His chief courtier Thomas Cromwell had persuaded the King to allow a complete English Bible, made by Tyndale's saintly colleague and collaborator, the former monk Miles Coverdale, to be sold openly and legally in England. Coverdale's 1535 version consisted of a revision of Tyndale's New Testament and Pentateuch, supplemented by Coverdale's own translation of the rest. Coverdale had no Greek or Hebrew, and his translations from Latin and German are arguably the more elegantly effective as a result: changing Tyndale's 'go in into thy master's joy', for instance, to 'enter thou into the joy of thy Lord'. He was the first printed translator to give us the Psalms (and thus 'the valley of the shadow of death', 'thy tender mercies and thy loving-kindnesses', and 'I will lift up mine eyes unto the hills'), which are retained in the Book of Common Prayer.

Two years after Coverdale's first Bible comes the so-called
Matthew's Bible of 1537, which – as I shamefully discovered only
last year – was printed by a merchant grocer called Richard Grafton
who gave his name to one of the houses of my school. Its editor
was John Rogers, chaplain to the Antwerp English community, and
the Bible is significant for the inclusion of a new version of the
history books of the Old Testament (Joshua to Chronicles), which
is convincingly attributed to Tyndale by his biographer, editor and
redoubtable champion David Daniell. More than doubling the
Tyndale Old Testament, these nine books may have been translated
in (and thus smuggled out from) Tyndale's prison cell. What is
certain is that – in an act of some generosity – Coverdale dropped
his own versions of these books, incorporating Tyndale's into the
subsequent versions he edited, including the extremely official
Great Bible of 1539.

By the time of his death, Henry VIII and his bishops had
backtracked on the Reformation and the English Bible, forbidding
its reading by men and women below the class of merchant and
gentlewoman, and banning entirely any Bible bearing Tyndale's
name (his *work* could not be banned without banning every English
Bible in print). But under the fervently Protestant Edward VI, the
Bible became central both to private and to public worship. As the
Catholic Church's missals and processionals and primers were
removed, the English Bible became the only source of doctrine and
ceremony. As the pictures, hangings, statues and even stained glass
were destroyed, the Scriptures were nailed up in their stead.

No wonder that the English Bible and its makers were regarded as
one of the cornerstones of the reform that Edward's elder sister
Mary sought to reverse when she became Queen in 1553. Miles
Coverdale sensibly fled England under Mary (returning after
Elizabeth's accession in 1558, and dying as an impoverished
country preacher). John Rogers, on the other hand, didn't leave
under Mary, and was the first of the nearly three hundred
Protestants to be burnt at the stake, at Smithfield, in sight of his
wife, with their eleventh child at her breast.

The remaining major Tudor translations were specifically doctrinal.
The 1560 Geneva Bible – which gave us 'the skin of my teeth',
'from strength to strength', 'vanity of vanities', 'unto us a child is
born' and 'my beloved son, in whom I am well pleased' – was
made in the Calvinist capital by Protestant exiles from Mary's reign
of terror (including Coverdale); was unfairly dismissed as 'the

breeches Bible' (for its description of Adam and Eve's post-Lapsarian covering); and is notable both for its scholarship and for its extensive and highly partial marginal notes. Twenty years later, with Protestant Elizabeth firmly on the throne, English Catholic exiles working from Douai and Rheims in France began producing a new Catholic English Bible, on the principle that if English translations were now unstoppable (and 'in the hands of every husbandman, artificier, prentice, boys, girls, mistress, maid') then they should at least get it right. The language is heavily Latinate: durable usages include 'adulterate', 'prescience' and 'verity', while 'potestates' and 'conculcation' failed to stick. Even so, Douai-Rheims gave us 'through a glass darkly', 'sufficient unto the day is the evil thereof', 'render unto Caesar the things that are Caesar's' and 'whited sepulchres'.

Douai-Rheims follows the 1568 Bishops' Bible, an attempt by Archbishop Matthew Parker to outflank Geneva by producing a Bible without 'bitter notes' or accidental 'lightness or obscenity' (no 'pissing she-mule', for instance), a Bible appropriate to the Elizabethan settlement, which sought to combine Catholic ceremonial with Protestant doctrine. Notably failing to supplant Geneva (the Bible of Spencer, Shakespeare and the Mayflower puritans), Bishops' is best known for its unfortunate rendering of 'cast thy bread upon the waters' as 'lay thy bread upon wet faces'. Nonetheless, it gave us 'be fruitful and multiply', 'spare the rod', 'the voice of one crying in the wilderness', 'kick against the pricks' and 'thou good and faithful servant'.

It was this Bible – printed unbound, for ease of distribution – which was given to the fifty-four scholars appointed by Archbishop Richard Bancroft to make yet another new translation in 1604. The project was a sop thrown to the puritan faction at a conference held by the newly acceded James I, at which – on all matters of substance – it had been defeated. In contrast to Tyndale, James did not believe in the monarchy as an alternative source of power to an overweening church; his slogan was 'No bishops, no king'. Less defensively – and despite the undoubted fillip given to the Protestant cause by the Gunpowder Plot the following year – James saw his great mission as keeping religious (and literal) peace in Europe, by bringing the warring factions of the Christian confession together.

Thus, and despite puritan support, the impetus of the translation was and remained deeply conservative, its aim to declare the English Reformation complete. The third striking thing – for me –

was the extent to which, doctrinally, the King James was not so much steady-as-she-goes as a pretty firm wrench on the tiller back towards the traditional religion. The establishment Bishops' Bible was the default text, there were to be no marginal notes, and the translators were instructed to defer to 'the ancient fathers', 'the analogy of the faith' and the 'old ecclesiastical words'. Thus, as Thomas More had insisted in the 1520s, Tyndale's 'elder', 'congregation' and 'love' were to be rendered as 'priest', 'church' and 'charity'. And, as contemporary critics pointed out, the KJB is surprisingly indebted to the Catholic Douai-Rheims version, following which the Protestant 'acknowledge' becomes the Catholic 'confess', 'ordinance' is rendered as 'tradition', and 'deeds' as the more papally freighted 'works'. It also seems to me that the KJB's liking for submission (to masters, husbands, kings, etc.) over Tyndale's preference for obeying, has a politics: submission is an acknowledgement of a prior hierarchy, obeying is something the individual chooses to do.

The Bible's divine authority was implied by an imposed uniformity of format and literary style (so poems like the Psalms and Mary's Magnificat in Luke are rendered in prose). For the 1611 reader, the Bible was overlaid with an antique patina: the increasingly outmoded 'thou' as the singular of 'you', the '-eth' ending to verbs as opposed to the current move to 's' ('hath' for 'has', 'doeth' for 'does'), 'thereof' for the contemporary 'its'. In his sonorous introduction, Bishop Miles Smith rejected slavish consistency, the idea that 'if we translate the Hebrew or Greek word once by purpose, never to call it intent; if once journeying, never travelling; if once think, never suppose; if once pain, never ache; if once joy, never gladness'; nonetheless, the KJB remains much more consistent in formulations like the Hebrew 'waw' (usually translated as 'and') than its predecessors. Analysing a passage of Genesis in which 'waw' appears thirty-four times, David Norton notes that Coverdale translates the word as 'and' on twenty-two occasions, Tyndale twenty-nine and the KJB thirty-one. The consistent – you could say persistent – use of conjunctive phrases like 'and it came to pass' (on which Tyndale rings the changes) gives the KJB a ritualised, almost plainsong feel. Following Bishops', colloquialisms were frowned on: Tyndale's serpent tells Eve 'Tush ye shall not die', King James's insists 'Ye shall not surely die'. And, while the word 'penance' does not appear in the 1611 Bible, in deference to the puritans, neither does the word 'tyrant', in deference to the King.

All of this said, the length and ease of the translation process, the advancement in Hebrew scholarship, and the diligence and distinction of the translators enabled them, time and again, to stand on their predecessors' shoulders. At the Stratford conference, it was tacitly forbidden to comment on the obvious upside of the translation's conservatism: its majesty and literary beauty. In that, we would have been at one with Miles Smith, who insisted that 'niceness in words was always counted the next step to trifling'. Nonetheless, it's no surprise that, building on 'their foundation that went before us', they often succeeded in making 'that better which they left so good'. So, the many memorable coinages which the translators selected (and often improved) from earlier versions are joined by many more that are original, from 'the root of the matter', 'a still small voice' and 'a thorn in the flesh', to 'lay up for yourselves treasures in heaven', 'get thee behind me, Satan', 'suffer little children' and 'let us now praise famous men'. The method of reading the translation out loud – and its purpose to be spoken – contributed to the creation of brilliant set pieces. The death of Jonathan in 2 Samuel ('how are the mighty fallen, and the weapons of war perished') is one of a number of passages in which scholarship combined with literary skill to turn clunky and even tortured phraseology into paragraphs of clarity, memorability and – yes – majesty.

Predictably, much time was spent in the *Written on the Heart* rehearsal room on the language. More surprising were increasingly passionate disputes about the doctrinal questions that the King James Bible was intended to resolve. I was brought up in what I realise in retrospect was a sternly Protestant school (its motto the monosyllablic 'God Grant Grace'), while my director Greg Doran was educated by the Jesuits and named after a Benedictine abbot. As we worked on the play – even more when the actors started bringing back the fruits of their researches into the various factions of the Reformation period – jokey disputes about the relative merits and sufferings of the Protestant and Catholic factions hardened into real dissension about the fundamental questions of the time. Day after day, we were told of the stripped altars, the smashed windows, the headless statues and the eyeless Saints, the transformation of a rich and magnificent visual culture into something small and silent and, above all, monochrome. When we were invited to St Paul's to see their tiny Tyndale New Testament, lying nestling on a cushion in the Cathedral's Dickensian library, it was hard not to ask whether all that was worth it, just for this.

It's fashionable to pour scorn on the easy causality of the radicalised version of Whig history: the model in which the Reformation fired an arrow that flew with unerring certainty via the enlightenment and the industrial revolution into the bullseye of liberal democracy: the theory summed up in the formulation 'No Erasmus, no Rousseau; no Luther, no Locke' (and thus no Newton, Franklin, Mandela or Microsoft). And if that progression is a myth, if, indeed, religious literalism is the profoundest enemy of free inquiry and enlightenment, then what can justify the first act of the story, that thirty years during which England moved from a state in which the English Bible was forbidden, to one in which it was compulsory; from a Church filled with glorious display of everything except the Word, to one in which the Word was all there was?

And yet. For all the sacrifices and the contradictions of the Protestant revolution, was not the move from a visual to a verbal culture, and, most of all, from the image to the book, a vital precondition for the creation of the modern world? Surely, the book gives us two things essential to intellectual progress. The first is easy communication of things, and with people, which you can't see. Visual culture is essentially an activity of present witness: yes, you can look at pictures of Naples or the Nile or Notre Dame, but before photography such images were cumbersome and expensive. The book is cheap and mass and mobile.

But second, the limitation of the book – its reliance on second-hand description of sights unseen – is what gives a verbal culture its particular power. The Chorus in *Henry V* instructs us to 'think, when we talk of horses, that you see them'. The book invites, indeed requires us to imagine, not just things which aren't there, but things that don't yet exist. In that sense, the book is as much a visual medium as the statue or the picture; with the difference that while the image invites you to lie back and enjoy it, the imagination requires us to sit up and join in with the work. Whatever their intentions, those first translators of the Bible into the vernacular gave us a means of communication and imagination which led – whether they liked it or not – to a world in which their own beliefs could be questioned and rejected. Or, if you like: no Tyndale, no Kindle.

The gap between the intention of the English Bible translators and the outcome of their work is as stark in the twenty-first century as it was in the seventeenth. When, in a 2004 speech on Britishness,

Gordon Brown praised the King James Bible for bringing different denominations 'together in committee to create a symbol of unity for the whole nation', he didn't mention that it failed. In fewer than ten years, Europe would be aflame with what was to become the Thirty Years War; within thirty, the English Civil War had broken out, consigning Archbishop Bancroft's successor William Laud and James's second son Charles to the executioner's block, an outcome chillingly predicted by Laud's patron, the translator Lancelot Andrewes, to Laud's face. And despite Laud's efforts to protect the KJB commercially by banning its competitors, the universal success of the King James version in England had to wait for the restoration of the monarchy, and its spread across the world for Britain's great imperial advance.

By which time, of course, a work written in and for a specific time, elbowing out previous versions on which it substantially relied, with many wonderful coinages as well as some pedestrian and repetitive formulations, had turned into something impossibly universal and apparently divinely provenanced, a book of which the proverbial American Baptist could insist: 'if it's good enough for St Paul, it's good enough for me'.

DAVID EDGAR

This is a revised version of an article published in the Guardian *on 19 February 2011.*

David Edgar
ALBERT SPEER
ARTHUR & GEORGE *after* Barnes
CONTINENTAL DIVIDE
EDGAR: SHORTS
THE MASTER BUILDER *after* Ibsen
PENTECOST
THE PRISONER'S DILEMMA
THE SHAPE OF THE TABLE
TESTING THE ECHO
A TIME TO KEEP *with* Stephanie Dale

Kevin Elyot
THE DAY I STOOD STILL
ELYOT: FOUR PLAYS
FORTY WINKS
MOUTH TO MOUTH
MY NIGHT WITH REG

Debbie Tucker Green
BORN BAD
DIRTY BUTTERFLY
RANDOM
STONING MARY
TRADE & GENERATIONS
TRUTH AND RECONCILIATION

Ayub Khan-Din
EAST IS EAST
LAST DANCE AT DUM DUM
NOTES ON FALLING LEAVES
RAFTA, RAFTA...

Liz Lochhead
BLOOD AND ICE
DRACULA *after* Stoker
EDUCATING AGNES ('The School for Wives') *after* Molière
GOOD THINGS
MARY QUEEN OF SCOTS GOT HER HEAD CHOPPED OFF
MEDEA *after* Euripides
MISERYGUTS & TARTUFFE *after* Molière
PERFECT DAYS
THEBANS

A Nick Hern Book

Written on the Heart first published in Great Britain in 2011 as a paperback original by Nick Hern Books Limited, 14 Larden Road, London W3 7ST, in association with the Royal Shakespeare Company

Written on the Heart copyright © 2011 David Edgar
Afterword and chronology copyright © 2011 David Edgar

David Edgar has asserted his moral right to be identified as the author of this work

Cover illustration by Emmanuel Polanco
Cover design by Ned Hoste, 2H

Typeset by Nick Hern Books, London
Printed in the UK by Mimeo Ltd, St Ives, Cambs PE27 3LE

A CIP catalogue record for this book is available from the British Library

ISBN 978 1 84842 207 0

MIX
Paper from
responsible sources
FSC® C019549
www.fsc.org